On Failing

Literary Activism

Series Editor: Amit Chaudhuri

On Failing

Edited by

Amit Chaudhuri

ashoka UNIVERSITY

CENTRE FOR
The Creative and
The Critical

First published by Westland Books, a division of Nasadiya Technologies Private Limited, in 2025

No. 269/2B, First Floor, 'Irai Arul', Vimalraj Street, Nethaji Nagar, Alapakkam Main Road, Maduravoyal, Chennai 600095

Westland and the Westland logo are the trademarks of Nasadiya Technologies Private Limited, or its affiliates.

ISBN: 9789360451998

10 9 8 7 6 5 4 3 2 1

Typeset by Jojy Philip, New Delhi

Printed at Parksons Graphics Pvt. Ltd

A Note on the Series

'Literary activism' is a project that began in 2014 with a series of annual symposia. Its aim was to create a space for the kind of discussion on creativity no longer available in mainstream contexts (literary festivals, book launches) or in academic ones (conferences, classrooms, monographs). The literary activism website—literaryactivism.com—was created in 2020, and the Centre for the Creative and the Critical at Ashoka University came into existence in 2022 to give this project a home, and to look at the kind of thinking that writing and the arts comprise.

This new imprint, 'literary activism', is meant to carry forward these ambitions in the realm of publishing. The art vs science debate is now a historical relic, but what interests us is the possibility of creating a meaning for writing that's separate from market value and academic legitimacy. And we wish to recall that art and writing are not synonymous with the generalised academic discipline called the 'humanities': they have an angularity to it, and to the social science perspectives the humanities are now subsumed under. The 'literary activism' imprint wishes not only to publish good writing, but to pursue this angularity.

On Failing: Mission Statement

The fifth symposium in the UEA 'literary activism' series took place on 14–15 February 2020 in partnership with Ashoka University at the India International Centre, New Delhi.

What is it that draws us to failing? We might not consciously *want* to fail, but, if we're engaged in creative practice, might unconsciously develop, over time, measures to protect ourselves from what Pound called 'SINGLE AND UNIQUE SUCCESS'. The free market, in the last twenty-five years, might have exhibited to us the importance of success—that success is not good fortune or a reward for accomplishment, but basic survival—and we might conspire to succeed only to a degree that's necessary for us to fail: because we know that it's only by failing that we can produce viable work, and only by succeeding to some extent that we can have the freedom to be non-viable. Failure has not only no dignity in the post-free market world we inhabit; it has no legitimacy, no vocabulary for self-appraisal. There are no actual 'alternative spaces' in the free market. Where do we locate ourselves, then, if we're to speak about 'failing'? For millennia we learnt from failure, and from failures: what do we make of that antithetical way of estimating significance? Various conceptions of form have, across cultures, embodied the liberations of failing: synecdoche; the image; metaphor—all these arise from a preferred inability to represent fully. Failure creates immediacy. This symposium asks participants to account for the attractions specific to failing; for why, and how, it awakens our desire; why it is taboo today in a way quite different from the by-no-means unbroken era before the market; and to reassess this history.

Amit Chaudhuri

Suicide as a Sort of Failure

Clancy Martin

I

'You know what's funny? Your jail anklet saved your life. They should put that in an advertisement! They should get a testimonial from you. If it weren't for that anklet, you'd be dead right now.'

I came to in a hospital bed with a sore head. I reached into my hair and felt the staples in my scalp. A handsome, young, dark-haired doctor with a bushy moustache and brightly lit, amused eyes, was standing by the side of my bed conversing cheerfully with me. I didn't know how long he'd been talking or if I had been talking back. I seemed to be joining the conversation midstream, but that may have been his manner. Perhaps he simply launched into conversation with his patients and let them catch up when they were ready.

I was very thirsty and still nervously fingering those metal staples.

I reached with my free hand for a large plastic cup of water that was on a bedside table. Then I realised that I was handcuffed to the bed.

'Here, let me get that for you.'

He tucked the bottle between the bed rail and the pillow, and bent the plastic straw into my mouth.

I drank the water and then spat out the straw. My throat was burning.

'Did I have an operation?' I asked.

'No, you were very lucky. Two minor procedures.'

He reached over to gesture at my head, where my staples and my fingers were.

'You must have fallen at some point. Your head was bleeding. Quite a nasty cut.'

'My throat hurts more than my head. My voice—' I said '—I sound awful. I don't feel sick.'

'We had to pump your stomach, but basically, you're fine. I'm so sorry we have to shackle you. They'll transfer you to the psychiatric ward tomorrow and then the security won't be necessary. You ruined your fancy anklet.'

He laughed. He was a very likeable doctor.

'It seems to have short-circuited, but not before it sent off its alarm. Modern technology.'

I wanted to explain about my anklet, but I realised that any extra details from me would sound defensive and anyway were superfluous.

'Next time, don't get in the bath. Better yet, don't have a next time, would you? We'd like to keep you around. And if you want to kill yourself don't use pills. Nobody dies from overdosing on pills anymore. The best way'—this is my doctor talking—'the best way is to duct tape a plastic bag around your head. There is even a book you can buy that tells you how—then tie up your hands before you run out of air. That'll do it. But you know, you were very lucky, and most people wise up after one attempt. So maybe this can be your get-out-of-jail-free card. That's how I'd approach it.'

I knew the book he meant. It's called *Final Exit* and I don't recommend it.

'You take care, try to behave yourself. Things will get better.' The doctor grabbed my foot, shook it gently, even affectionately, shrugged his shoulders and left the room.

I thought, well, that was kind of nice. That was a much more pleasant encounter than you expected with a doctor after you'd tried suicide. That guy ought to be training others on how to deal with the situation.

I had an IV in my arm, and while there was a phone by the bed, I couldn't reach it because it was on the handcuffed side. I had a nurse alert button by my hand but I didn't want to beep a nurse to help me make a phone call.

'Three weeks ago I was in bed at home with my girlfriend,' I said out loud theatrically to the empty hospital room. I wouldn't have done it if I weren't alone. 'Three weeks ago, everything was normal,' I said.

But it wasn't the truth. My life had been abnormal for a long time.

They woke me up in the middle of the night to transfer me to Research Psychiatric. It was quiet in the ward. Everyone was asleep. In 2009, 2010 and 2011, during the three worst years of my adulthood (thus far), I had had extraordinarily vivid dreams, and I loved to dream because I often dreamt of my children and other good things that were no longer real in my waking everyday life.

This particular suicide attempt was in the winter of 2010.

'Can't we go in the morning?'

They took the handcuffs off my wrists but stood very close to me as I got out of bed.

'We don't decide when you get transferred. Your ambulance is here. You're going to the psychiatric ward.'

'Why an ambulance?' I asked the ambulance fellows downstairs at the doors. 'Can't we just take a car?'

Despite the frigid winter air, the truth was that it was walking distance, maybe two blocks. It's all on the same hospital campus.

'It's a liability thing—you'll get a bill for it. You're not going to try to run on us, right?' the EMT said.

I was in my hospital robe, in slippers and shivering. It was very cold outside where the ambulance was waiting. They wrapped a strange padded vinyl silver blanket around me. I was hot immediately.

The field beyond the parking lot was covered in snow. The stars were bright. I thought: That's what I'd like to be; as far away and indifferent as something in the night sky.

'Run where?'

'You can sit up here with us,' the other EMT said. 'It's not strictly according to regulations but what the hell.'

It was a bench seat and I sat in the middle between the driver and his partner.

'It's like *Bringing Out the Dead*,' I said. 'Did you guys ever see that movie?'

'Uh-uh,' the driver said. The other one said, 'I think I saw it.'

'If you saw it you'd remember,' I said. 'It's about an ambulance driver. Nicolas Cage.'

'And he sees ghosts, right?' the driver said. He had a beard and looked about twenty years old.

'That's it! You did see it.'

I paused for a second. We were pulling up to the psychiatric building.

'You guys ever see any ghosts?' I asked.

I think suicidal people can see into the world of ghosts in a way that sturdier folks cannot. The Canadian addiction expert Gabor Maté describes alcoholics like me as 'living in the realm of hungry ghosts': people who have become ghosts while still alive. And I think you can almost see when a deeply addicted person who is killing himself with his drug of choice is making the transition into the ghost lands.

'Not Scorsese's best,' the driver said, ignoring or avoiding my question. 'I always thought *Goodfellas* was his real masterpiece.'

'Or *Raging Bull*,' I said. 'That's one of the saddest movies ever made.'

'I've seen a couple of ghosts!' the guy on my right said. 'People see them. It's a real thing. My aunt once had a ghost ask if it could kiss her. A *female* ghost.'

'No one wants to hear that bullshit,' the driver said briskly, interrupting his buddy. 'We're here. At the *psychiatric* hospital,' he said, giving the ghost guy a pointed look.

They put me in the tiny claustrophobic office just off the main waiting room. It was I'd guess four or five in the morning.

A thirty-something slender, pale intake nurse asked me: 'Are you feeling suicidal right now? Are you having suicidal thoughts?'

I don't know why but I was honest with her. Maybe I was still high from the Benadryl they'd given me at the hospital to keep me calm, or maybe I was at the end of my rope.

'Well, glad you asked. If you leave me alone in here, I will slash my wrists with your scissors, I will hang myself with the blinds, I will electrocute myself with a fucking fork. Yes. What do you think?'

'If you're feeling violent ... are you threatening me? Are you thinking of attacking me?'

She picked up the phone. I noticed she had chubby hands and fingers that tapered down like pyramids. She had a no-nonsense expression and an all-American appearance, with clean nicely brushed brown hair. She was young and looked like she could have been one of my oldest daughter's friends, and I regretted what I had said. She was just doing her job.

'No, I'm not feeling violent. I apologise. I'm not having suicidal thoughts.'

I had forgotten to lie about what I was thinking, which is the cardinal rule of intensive psychiatric care. It's like the 'deny, deny, deny' rule for adulterers; with psychiatrists, 'lie, lie, lie' is the only way to survive. The only hope is of getting out of there.

'I just want to sleep. I'm freezing. Are you cold? It's freezing in here.'

I still had the too-hot silver blanket from the EMTs but it was cold in her office, and I was in the mood to complain. I was in the hospital robe. I'd lost the slippers and was barefoot.

'I'm sorry about the temperature, sir, but I would appreciate if you would try to use civil language with me. What have they done with your clothes?'

'I need some socks. I don't have any clothes. They found me in a bathtub.'

'Oh, I see.' This did not dismay or even surprise her. In fact, it seemed to reassure her. Like now we were making some progress. She typed it into her computer.

'Well, there's a bed opening in the morning in the annex. I think you'll have to wait for a few hours. Here, we'll finish your paperwork and you're welcome to take a nap in the waiting room if you like. I'll find you a real blanket. You should have someone bring you down some clothes.'

'Can I make a phone call? I'm sure I can have someone come right away. That would be really helpful actually.'

The white office phone sat there on her desk. Her cell phone was beside it.

'No.'

'No?'

'I'm afraid not.'

Unlike when you're arrested, when they whisk you off to the madhouse there is no guaranteed right to a phone call.

'Okay. I guess I'll wait in the waiting room.'

She went to get me another blanket and I heard her lock the door behind me. She took her cell phone with her and when I tried to dial an outside line on her desk phone I couldn't get through. They requested a security code. I sat back down in my chair when I heard her at the door. She gave me an irritated suspicious look when she came into the room.

'There's a camera right there,' she said, and pointed to the corner above her desk.

She handed me a red cotton blanket, and some blue cotton slippers that looked like they had been left behind by another patient. They were too fuzzy to be institutional slippers.

'You're going to have to wait in here.'

I watched the door closed behind her and immediately regretted not making a run for it when they were putting me in the ambulance. Those guys were bigger than I am, and no doubt faster, but I could have found a place to hide. Dejected, I put the red blanket around my chest like a towel under the silver blanket, so that I'd be more comfortable, and then on impulse I stood up abruptly and tried the nurse's office door. It was locked.

I startled her. She started to rise from her desk.

'Do you need to go to the restroom?'

'Yes,' I said, 'please.'

Okay, this was my chance. There were a few chairs in the little waiting room and a security guard was talking to a nurse or orderly who sat behind a desk behind a counter with a sliding glass front like a doctor's office. The door out had a big metal push bar.

It was a frozen Kansas City winter night, but if I were free, there would be opportunities. Something would present itself.

This is how I thought at that time. Everything was one second to the next. I couldn't conceive of tomorrow. Things were just happening; and they were either good or bad. I wanted to get away from the bad things and find the good things. Or, if there were no good things to find, kill myself. To get away altogether. It was like the opposite of what William Blake and Søren Kierkegaard might have been talking about when they wrote about the bliss of immediacy and mystical experience. I had a kind of immediacy of despair, I suppose. Or I just couldn't bear to think more than a few minutes ahead because I knew what was coming.

I twisted away from her and ran for the door.

She said 'Sir' and the security guard turned, but I was too quick for them. He didn't have time to get up.

I've made it! Bang! Hit the metal bar, dropped my silver blanket.

The door was locked. I pushed against it again with my whole body, for a moment imagining liberty. I rested my forehead on the cold glass.

Then I turned around, shrugged and tried to act like it was their fault.

'Why did you do that?'

'I'm sorry,' I said. I knew I had betrayed her trust. Plus, I was stealing her slippers.

'Do you still need to use the restroom?'

They didn't say anything else about it. I expected some kind of formal reprimand, and even perhaps a punishment or restraints, but it was like it never happened. I supposed it must happen more often than you think.

'Yes, I need to use the bathroom,' I said.

There was a door with a men–women–wheelchair sign on it. I went into it and saw there was no lock. They had everything figured out: there was no air duct you might climb into like in a movie, just a sturdy looking fluorescent light panel in the ceiling and nothing I could use to kill myself.

I sat on the toilet and cried.

I stopped and looked in the mirror.

They had a normal mirror, not a stainless steel one like you find in many institutional settings. It was the one thing you might use to kill yourself with. I could smash the mirror and slash myself with a shard of glass. If I had been a different person, I could perhaps have used a shard of glass to menace someone into an escape, but all of my fight was exhausted by my useless dash for the door.

I was defeated, and anyway, I doubted I could break the mirror if I tried. In the mirror to myself, in my great self-pity at that moment, I looked like I was about twelve years old.

I wiped the tears off my face and for a moment, relaxed the armour of irony about my ridiculous situation. I let myself feel very, very sorry for myself. My eyes were large and red. My face was still pink from the cold and I wanted my mom. My hair was freshly washed for my stitches and my bangs were tousled and boyish. I was momentarily inspired and reassured by the childishness of my own desperation.

And there I was. I walked back out of the bathroom to try to face whatever was coming my way next.

II

One of the reasons that suicide makes us uncomfortable is that it is a very public confession of failure.

In fact, there may be no more complete confession of failure that a person can make both to herself and the world than trying to take their own life. It's kind of like a last desperate shout-out to the world: 'Okay, I admit it, I'm a failure! You beat me! You won!'

Even among the philosophers who allow suicide as a legitimate and even noble means of escaping evil, such as Cicero, it is generally recommended to those who either find themselves in the midst of failure or as a desirable action given the failures that were to come.

In fact, on Cicero's account, as obsessed with the problem of failure as he is, you've failed both yourself and your friends by failing to kill yourself in circumstances of failure, but failed even worse if you choose to live and fail to properly anticipate the failures to come. Suicide is not only an entirely appropriate response to failure, it is a sensible method of avoiding it.

Thus the worst paradox the suicide encounters if he attempts suicide and fails, he finds that now he has failed even in that. As the eventually successful David Foster Wallace remarked in an interview with *Rolling Stone*: 'I knew that if anybody was fated to fuck up a suicide attempt it was me, but if he succeeds at his suicide and shows everyone that finally he is not the fuck up everyone supposed him to be, well, no one looks at the suicide and thinks thank goodness, he got one thing right! And even if they did, he's not around to enjoy it!'

III

'Later, none of the guests at the party believed when they heard what happened. They were already thinking of suicide then.'

At this point in his novel *Suicide*, Levé's hero has not killed himself yet. He is at a party with old friends and for a change he seems to be genuinely happy.

If you don't know the story of the magnificent French writer and photographer Édouard Levé, he was born in 1965, studied business at an elite school in Paris, became an abstract painter, then burned all his work, took a transformational (as he described it) two-month trip to India and then took up his mature and robust career as a photographer and writer. His last book was the novel *Suicide*, which he wrote in 2007, gave to his editor and then promptly killed himself.

I recently had a friend visit from Los Angeles who had read an essay of mine about suicide and was interested in the question of why I am suicidal. We were driving around Kansas City together. I was showing him some of my old stomping grounds and he was interested in the city generally. As we passed the Nelson–Atkins Museum of Art heading towards the campus of University of Missouri-Kansas City, he said: 'Either you're really happy now, happy to be with Amie and your kids and a very long way from wanting to kill yourself or you're the best actor I have ever met.'

I agreed that I was happy and that I was a long way from killing myself (which, most days, I think I am) although I also told him that it was all very fragile, that Amie could leave me or something else could go wrong in my life and suddenly I'd be back on the edge, which is also entirely true, I think.

The point of course is that being happy and thinking of suicide then as Levé writes above are not at all incompatible. That's not only because one might see one's happiness as an exception to the rule, a pleasant but surely brief surprise. It's also not only because there seems to be for a lot of us a deeper underlying happiness that persists even in cheerful psychologically stable times.

Once you have the habit of thinking you are going to kill yourself, that habit doesn't necessarily go away. A Buddhist Lama I study under, Dzongsar Khyentse Rinpoche, writes in his book *Living Is Dying* that suicide is habit-forming through lifetimes and that the urge to kill oneself is often just the expression of having killed oneself in a previous life. You don't want to do a reductio ad absurdum on that one, but anyway, it had to start somewhere. Therefore, he teaches, it is important to break the habit now, rather than reinforcing it again.

Of course, for Buddhists any habit breaking—even the breaking of good habits—is generally encouraged. Some Buddhists argue that the suffering that comes from our confusion about reality is primarily a consequence of our habits. For me the habit of suicide was mentally ingrained years before I actually, sincerely, physically tried to kill myself.

So when I think of killing myself now, it's a lot like thinking of taking a drink, it's not attractive, it doesn't have the allure but it feels both familiar and real. And I suppose it's fair to say that it somehow even feels natural.

I have an email friend who writes to me sometimes about her desire to kill herself, and she says that suicide feels inevitable to her. When I push back, she agrees that it's not inevitable, but I know just what she's talking about. It's that same feeling of naturalness, of the ease of the thought. If I think about taking a jog it sounds more troublesome, more psychologically difficult or irritating to me than killing myself does, and this despite the fact that I really love jogging, though I still have not formed the habit.

On the car ride to a conference in 2020, just before COVID broke out, I was discussing suicide with Amit Chaudhuri and Sumana Roy, and Amit said: 'I think it would be so upsetting not to have the thought of suicide go through your mind from time to time. Then there would be no way out!' And it's true that when friends or students or readers of mine come to me to talk about their suicidal feelings, I almost always give them a variation of what I will now always call Amit's consolation: 'Look, everyone feels that way sometimes, and if you can just keep going today you can always still kill yourself tomorrow.'

Of course, sometimes the sheer pressure of the thought of suicide, the claustrophobia of the walls of that thought coming ever closer to you, is itself part of the panic that leads to the suicide attempt.

When Levé considers the familiarity of the thought of suicide, his narrator describes himself as a biological failure. 'You were perhaps a weak link, an accidental evolutionary dead end, a temporary anomaly not destined to burgeon again.'

Which reminds me of the line from the CIA agent Dan who tortures detainees in the movie *Zero Dark Thirty*. 'It's cool that you're strong and I respect it, I do,' he tells his victim, 'but in the end everybody breaks, bro. It's biology.'

IV

There are lots of ways in which Levé's nameless hero and suicide seem familiar to me and will be familiar to other suicidal people. Perhaps most intimately, he doesn't expect to be happy, but looks for ways to suffer less and makes his decisions using this criterion. He tells himself, 'You directed at yourself a violence that you did not feel toward others.'

I've often asked my students: 'Imagine what your life would be like if you had the same contempt for others that you have for yourself.' This to help them see that others do not have the contempt for them that they might suspect, and also to see hopefully that their own self-contempt is unjustified and probably unnecessary.

Certainly, we don't judge other people as harshly as we judge ourselves.

I also worry that the desire to kill myself is an expression of my anger at other people, that it is a lashing out against the people I love. Certainly, most suicides are interpreted that way, at least in some measure, and of course Freud's analysis of suicide is that it is just a displaced murder. We want to kill someone else but we dare not, and so, like the drive for cruelty turning back upon itself in

Nietzsche's story about the creation of human consciousness, the murderous hand becomes a *sélbstmord*, the poetic German word for suicide.

But if I think of the times I actually tried to kill myself, or even of the wistful worry I have now that it might be better off to, that I might be better off dead, I see that the violence of the idea—if indeed it must be violent, which it somehow doesn't seem that way in imagination—is in fact not directed at anyone else at all, or if it is an attempt to punish someone else, it is more like the punishment enacted on Shia LaBeouf by his father in the autobiographical movie *Honey Boy*, when his dad tells him, 'Nobody is mad at me anymore, that's all I ever wanted.'

Yes, it's a model of self-pity, but we understand this feeling sorry for ourselves and wanting other people to feel sorry for us too, and if we aren't murdering someone else when we kill ourselves, at least hurting them because they don't feel sorry enough for us, might be part of our motivation.

'Your mother cried for you when she learned of your death,' Levé writes. In this very lean novel, the hero's mother gets a full paragraph of crying over her dead son. She cries and cries and cries, and which one of us thinking of suicide hasn't shamefacedly dared to hope for that. One of the consoling thoughts about dying (and at times, some of the motivation for suicide) is the hope that our mothers, at least, will cry. This is not just Levé's wish-fulfilment, it also gives us one of the keys to the text, which is that Levé is telling us something about the psychology of the suicidal person; showing us not the world the way it really is, despite our wish as the usual job of the novelist, but the way the world is dreamt of in the fantasy of the suicidal person.

His paragraph about the mother's tears, coming very near the end of the novel as it does, is a mockery of the suicide, but it is a melancholy, sympathetic mockery, and of course also a self-mockery, the kind of self-irony at which the suicidal person perhaps excels. We can both make fun of the fact that we want our mothers to cry at our funerals, and very much want our mothers to cry at our funerals, and even kill ourselves just so that we can be assured of our mothers crying at our funerals, which otherwise is not very likely to happen.

(It's a funny paradox about being a parent that despite protesting sincerely that we would do anything for our children, none of us would be willing to live longer than them.)

'Years later,' Levé writes, 'there are many like her whose tears flow whenever they think of you.' Exaggerated, dramatic and just the kind of sentimental flourish that the suicide engages in when thinking about his own demise. It sounds a little like our hero at the beginning of this talk who looked at himself in the mirror and cried tears over the piteousness of his own situation.

The final paragraph of Levé's book strikes a different tone and is a powerful counterbalance to the teary self-pitying paragraph that precedes it.

'Regrets? You had some for causing the sadness of those who cried for you ...' (it's worth remembering that this is all being written by a man who was about to kill himself and has tried to kill himself before) '... for the love they felt for you and which you had returned. You had some for the solitude in which you left your wife and for the emptiness your loved ones would experience, but these regrets, you felt merely in anticipation, they would disappear along with you. Your survivors would be alone in carrying the pain of your death. The selfishness of your suicide displeased you, but all things considered the lull of death won out over life's painful commotion.'

It's true that his suicide is selfish, as indeed are many suicides. In some ways suicide is the most selfish act one can perform. It is a kind of wholly taking something that belongs to many people, and making it entirely yours alone. It's burning down a house in which many people live just because *I* don't want to live there anymore. There's no point trying to hide from, or gloss over, the selfishness of suicide.

He wasn't trying to hide from his selfishness. Every verse in the poem that concludes the novel ends with 'me' or contains 'my', 'this', 'me', 'me', 'my', 'my', 'I.'

I is both the suicide's refrain, and one reason we are suspicious of the suicide and perhaps angry with him after the fact. Angry at him whether he tried and failed to kill himself, and angry at him if he tried and succeeded. But it might also make us suspicious of people who try to hide from their own selfishness. We are right to rebuke the suicide 'you were unforgivably selfish'—but that also means 'You are much more selfish than I am.'

When Mary Carr heard the news of her friend and lover David Foster Wallace's successful suicide she wrote, 'Every suicide's an asshole. There is a good reason I am NOT God for I would cruelly smite the self-smitten.' But on whose behalf are we self-righteously indignant? Who is feeling sorry for who now, and who's better off—the dead suicide who was in too much pain to go on living, or the living one who is in more pain now that the friend is gone?

When David Foster Wallace writes that the suicide is like someone jumping from a burning building, he is perhaps not so much trying to excuse the suicide, as explain the action he is taking, and perhaps to reply to those people who would accuse the suicide of monstrous selfishness. Of course the person leaping from a burning building is doing something selfish, Wallace might tell us, but she is doing a selfish thing any of us would do if our suffering were similar to hers. It is a selfishness we have to be able to understand, and even sympathise with.

The problem with the metaphor of course is that the person in the burning building dies either way, it's just one death is less painful than the other. And it's true that we all die either way but the family and friends of the suicide can reasonably reply, 'You didn't have to die yet.'

'Couldn't you have endured the suffering for us and perhaps we could have even found a way to help with the suffering, because after all, you weren't always suffering like that, and there is a reason to believe that maybe you wouldn't always have to?'

But it's also hard to get past the recognition (or the hope) of the lull of death when you're dead. Yes, the ones behind will have things a bit harder, a bit worse than they do now and you will have caused that, but they are still in life's painful commotion and you've exited.

In killing myself, were I, especially as a parent, to do it, I have to accept that the ones I leave behind may do as I have done. Which reminds me of my psychiatrist Grace Kellerman's admonition to me: 'Don't not kill yourself because of your children, your children will miss you but in the end they'll be fine. Don't kill yourself because of the example you'd be setting for them.'

That's a very good reason not to kill yourself, if you have children: one of the best reasons I've ever heard. Wallace, who had no children, understood this point. In *The Pale King*, the novel which was interrupted by his suicide, several of the characters are considering suicide and one of them, Lane Dean Jr., always manages to stop himself by looking at a picture of his newborn child.

On 12 September 2008, David Foster Wallace hanged himself on the patio of his home in Claremont, California. His first suicide attempt that we know of was about twenty years before, at his parents' home in Urbana where he grew up. He overdosed on a tranquiliser, followed by a stay in a psychiatric hospital in the course of ECT treatments for depression. He made one more suicide attempt that we know of for certain; also an overdose before his death.

It started early for Wallace. He was already writing about suicide as a teenager and his first attempt was in his early twenties. In a letter to his lifelong friend Jonathan Franzen when he was twenty-eight, he writes that suicide is 'a reasonable if not at this point a desirable option with respect to the whole wretched problem'. In a story from around the same time, he writes:

> You are the sickness yourself. You realise all this when you look at the black hole and it's wearing your face. That's when the bad thing just absolutely eats you up or rather when you just eat yourself up. When you kill yourself. All this business about people committing suicide when they're severely depressed, we say holy cow we must do something to stop them from killing themselves, that's wrong, because all these people have, you see, by this time already killed themselves where it really counts. When they commit suicide they're just being orderly.

But all this is just theory, Professor Wallace, what about when they try to kill themselves for real and fail?

One of the paradoxes of the failed suicide is that he starts feeling like an imposter—a pretender—a joke. People want to ask him: 'You've tried repeatedly, how come you haven't managed it yet? Get your act together!' But of course the struggle isn't killing yourself so much as not killing yourself!

Wallace summarises it this way: 'So cry all you want. I won't tell anybody. But it wouldn't have made you a fraud to change your mind. It would be sad to do it because you think you somehow have to.'

We'd be lying if we failed to acknowledge the theatrical character of the kind of self-pitying person the suicidal person is. Wallace signed his letters to Mary Carr 'Young Werther,' the most famous fictional suicide in Western literature. Andrew Solomon wrote of his approach to suicide that he knew he was in real trouble when he could no longer distinguish between his drama over his depression and his depression itself. (It's something to remember if you're wrestling with depression: when you're at that point where you can no longer distinguish between your depression and your drama over your depression make sure you get some help.)

The summer before David Foster Wallace finally succeeded in killing himself he tried and failed again at overdosing on pills. And those of us who have failed at suicide through overdosing on pills (it is in fact the most common way of failing to kill yourself) know the secret that we don't like to admit, which is that suicide is scary. And we might be a bit cowardly. It's scary to think that now it's time to die, and it's also scary to think of ways of doing it that might be really painful. If suicide is the coward's way out, as people angry over a suicide like to say, failing at suicide is cowardice squared! Too cowardly to live but also too cowardly to die.

But then David Foster Wallace found his courage. His partner said at the time that: 'Saturday was a really good day. Monday and Tuesday were not so good. He started lying to me that Wednesday.' Two days went by but she was a little less worried than usual because on that Monday this difficult fellow—who hated to go to the doctor despite having spent much of his adult life in the care of various doctors—had been willing to go to the chiropractor.

'You don't go to the chiropractor if you're going to commit suicide,' she said. That is probably true, and probably, on Monday, Wallace still didn't know that it would be his last week with his wife. He was still fighting against suicide then, still going through the motions required of life. He had courage enough to live on Monday, and by Wednesday he had courage enough to buy the rope that he would use to hang himself on Friday.

In the previously mentioned interview with *Rolling Stone*, Wallace described a time when he successfully stopped himself from killing himself. 'I got really worried I was going to kill myself.' He walked across campus to health services—this was when he was at Harvard—and told a psychiatrist: 'Look, there's this issue, I don't feel real safe.'

'It was a big deal for me because I was so embarrassed,' Wallace said, 'but it was the first time I ever treated myself like I was worth something.' They checked him into a psychiatric hospital, the same one where the failed suicide Robert Lowell once stayed, and then the failed and then successful suicide Sylvia Plath also stayed.

'When that happens to you,' Wallace went on, smiling at the interviewer, 'you get unprecedentedly willing to examine other alternatives for how to live.'

The writer Sumana Roy once asked: 'When is failure ever expected?' And when trying to kill ourselves, though we may paradoxically hope to fail, if we are trying at all, we are expecting to succeed.

I was recently talking to a philosopher friend of mine about a suicide attempt he'd made when he was eighteen. He said you know all that about how if you tried it but didn't actually manage to do it, how everybody thinks you didn't really mean it?' 'A cry for help,' I said. 'Yeah, but I don't think that's true at all. Because when I woke up and realised I had failed, I was absolutely gutted.'

If you talk to people in psychiatric hospitals immediately following their suicide attempts, as I have done many times, you know that this is a common report. No one in there is celebrating the *gift of being alive*.

And yet when you realise that at every moment, you could kill yourself, if you chose to, then in a funny way every moment you are alive becomes this astonishing triumph. This is a thought that is so obvious that we fail to appreciate its importance: you don't have to be here.

It's so hard to be here, and yet here you are! You grossly underestimate yourself. You might remember in Philip Roth's prophetic novel *The Human Stain*, perhaps his best novel about failure and wilful self-destruction, the existentialist imperative Roth offers us in the words of his hero is the simple plea repeatedly made to his lover: 'Keep on dancing.'

I think of Pratap Mehta's work and his idea of the redemptive power of spontaneous action, which is so well and frequently expressed through the metaphors of music and dancing. I think of those unjustly vilified forms of the aesthetic: disco music and disco dancing, and especially the Bee Gees. Also, I couldn't resist the appeal of putting Pratap Mehta and the Bee Gees in the same paragraph.

You know when they teach you how to sustain or resuscitate a person in a CPR class, they teach you to palpate the chest to the beat of the Bee Gees song *Stayin' Alive*? And I think in this way we might try to understand and forgive the suicide who simply didn't have any more disco in him, and had to get off the dance floor to take a rest.

But also, we could congratulate ourselves and recognise that it's a victory every day we succeed in Staying Alive.

Description of a Poet's Failure

Ranajit Das

> 'Go on failing. Go on.
> Only next time, try to fail better'
>
> —Samuel Beckett

Some small wonders of life are its ironic surprises. My participation in this symposium is just such a surprise for me. At first, I was taken aback when my dear friend Amit Chaudhuri, whose writings I greatly admire and who is perfectly aware of my utter ineligibility to take part in any scholarly discourse, suddenly made me an offer to deliver a talk in an august symposium to be held on the theme of 'Failure'. But then I quickly realised that it's an offer I cannot logically decline, because, being an elderly and obscure Bengali poet who has failed in his pursuit to achieve fame in his long poetic career, I can at least claim with some dignity that failure is my forte. Thus I agreed with a chuckle at myself, after making a quick mental calculation that my poor English might also go well with the drift of the subject itself.

So here I am, ladies and gentlemen, and here are some bare facts about myself. I have been writing poetry for the last fifty years, having published twelve books of poems, along with two collections of literary essays and one novel to my credit. And in the bargain, I have received some awards too. But in spite of such seemingly impressive biodata, not a single cultured and literature-loving Bengali bhadralok, outside the small literary circle of Bengali poetry, has heard of me. If you think it's an exaggeration, ask any respectable

Bengali gentleman in Kolkata whether he has heard of a poet called Ranajit Das and you are sure to meet with a sceptic frown and a glum response, 'Ranajit who?' Please don't think I am concocting stories to project my image in a comical light. Listen to this. Very recently, a journalist friend of mine, who is a senior assistant editor of a leading daily, did me a great favour by commissioning a short feature from me, no, not on any literary topic, but on film star Rekha on the occasion of her umpteenth birthday for his newspaper, and he published it with a prominent photograph of mine at the top corner of the feature.

My wife was elated to see her poor old husband's photograph at long last in a newspaper, and treated me to a sumptuous breakfast with my favourite cheese omelette. But my excitement was short-lived when a neighbour of mine met me at the bazaar and said, 'Hey, Mr Das, I have read in today's newspaper an interesting article on Rekha and Amitabh Bachchan! I forgot the writer's name, but the guy looks like you!' I stood crestfallen, as I realised that even photographic evidence in a prominent daily could not dispel my obscurity.

But there is an interesting fall-out. As you know, any long-standing obscurity of a poet gradually becomes a kind of fame in itself—a very stubborn, cultish, underground fame, which is always dreaded by celebrity-poets! Because this kind of clandestine fame is rumoured to have a direct link with immortality in the world of art. (It's a sinister and haunting rumour that tends to make the dead poets alive and the live poets dead!)

In any case, my own enduring obscurity has endowed me with a little bit of this dubious fame, and a group of young poets have become my loyal admirers. They believe that I have been deprived of my due share of fame by a literary culture dominated by aggressive self-promotion. One young poet admonished me with these words, 'Dada, you are such a powerful poet, but nobody knows your name. It's all your fault, why didn't you take care of your PR seriously?' I instantly replied, 'Listen, kid, being a genuine poet, I never had any interest in making PR, as I am only interested in making love!' But the boy was not amused, and he hit back, 'Dada, it's not a matter of your *ghatia* joke, because even God cannot survive without constant

PR in this world.' And then he delivered his punchline with a sarcastic smile, 'By the way, dada, could you find much success in your pursuit of love either?' This was a real hit below the belt, literally, because with my looks and my obscurity, I was a damn flop in that field as well. I sacrificed fame for the sake of love, and love ignored me for my lack of fame. I have got the worst of both worlds!

This, in short, is the description of my failure as a poet. Now the question is, leaving comedy apart, how do I view this failure myself? Am I okay with this failure? Or do I resent it? What kind of a failure is this? Until now, I have implied that this is only a failure to earn literary fame, and is totally unrelated to the question of quality of my poetry. It might even be surmised from my foregoing account that I have been taking a hidden pride in this failure, and covertly flaunting this failure as a feather in my cap of self-respect. And here comes the hard question. Did I actually fail to earn fame because I failed to write good poetry?

This question lies at the heart of the matter and opens up the whole issue, calmly indicating that an impartial judgement from the literary community about the quality of my poetry should be the deciding factor in the matter. For my part, I always dream of such a trial, in which the verdict is finally out that my poetry is indeed poor and therefore my failure is justified, and I accept this verdict with a humble and grateful heart. I almost feel relieved to get rid of a tormenting poetic ambition which is beyond me. I bow to the jury and step down from the dock. And then I politely recede from public view, never to be seen again. Conjuring up this image of myself as a failed and forlorn poet silently receding into literary oblivion gives me a strange catharsis from my fervent desires to achieve literary fame. I find in this image the faint prospect of a strange resurgence of a poet who has met, for the first time, the hard truth of his poetic failure, has been cast out of the garden of poetry, and retreated into a solitude of utter desolation from which he might still emerge as a true poet in his second birth. Because this solitude, like the proverbial ant-hill of the jungle-bandit Ratnakara, might prove for him the real creative solitude in which he might at last acquire the heart and the art of poetry.

And talking of failure, I must now recall the tragic life and majestic poetry of our 'Nirjanotamo kabi' (the most lonely of poets) Jibanananda Das (1899–1954), the poet who was almost unknown during his lifetime, lived in utter misery, but wrote incredibly great poetry, and is now universally regarded as the greatest Bengali poet since Rabindranath Tagore. He was 'a painfully private person' (in the words of his American biographer Clinton B. Seely), who failed miserably in almost all spheres of his personal life, except his poetry. By profession he was a teacher of English literature, but he frequently lost his jobs owing to various reasons, including his own diffidence and reclusive nature, and serial cruelties of fate. He had a slight stammer, for which he faced occasional ridicule from his colleagues and students. Afflicted with a profound poetic indolence, he remained jobless for long periods, lived in abject poverty, and bore the brunt of an extremely unhappy family life, with a bitter and disgruntled wife and two children. All along his hapless life, he frantically looked for means to earn his living, mostly without success. Even a couple of years before his death, he went to the Writers' Building—the seat of the state government in Kolkata, in the hope of procuring a government permit to start some petty business, where he fainted and fell ill. Finally, he died in a tram accident in Kolkata in 1954. Speculation is still rife in the literary circle of Bengal that this accident might actually be an act of suicide.

I feel inclined to quote the touching description of the poet's death in Mr Seely's heartfelt words.

> Jibanananda had been in the habit of going for a walk, often by himself ... On the fateful evening, Jibanananda was returning home, heading north. Rashbehari Avenue, a major thoroughfare, had to be crossed before he could proceed the hundred yards or so back to his flat. Down the centre of Rashbehari run two tram lines. Of just such tram lines he had written some sixteen years earlier:
>
> *It is late—so very late at night.*
> *From one Calcutta sidewalk to another,*
> *from sidewalk to sidewalk*

As I walk along, my life's blood feels the vapid,
venomous touch
Of tram tracks stretched out beneath my feet like
A pair of primordial serpent sisters.
A soft rain is falling, the wind slightly chilling.
Of what far land of green grass, rivers, fireflies
Am I thinking?
Where are the stars?
Have those stars been lost?
Beneath my feet the slender tram track—
above my head a mesh of tangled wires
Chastises me

> A tramcar approached from the west as Jibanananda began to cross the road, and, *for some reason oblivious,* he stepped in front of it. Taken by taxi to Sambhunath Pandit Hospital, Jibanananda was treated for several broken ribs, a fractured clavicle, and one shattered leg. While at the hospital, Dr Bhumendra Guha, then a medical student and some of his fellow students from the Medical College were constantly at Jibanananda's side ... Dr Bidhan Chandra Roy, then chief Minister of West Bengal (was requested by a prominent well-wisher of the poet) to see personally to Jibanananda's care; Dr Roy came to the hospital the following day. Every effort was made to save his life. But Jibanananda contracted pneumonia, and on 22 October 1954, eight days after the accident, he died.[1] [Italics mine.]

This is how the tragic life of the great poet ended.

During his lifetime, only 162 of Jibanananda's poems were published. And even on the strength of these meagre number of poems, he was posthumously able to change the entire course of Bengali poetry from the hallowed mystic world of Tagore to the fractured psyche of modernity. Needless to say, he is now hailed as

[1] *A Poet Apart: A Literary Biography of the Bengali Poet Jibanananda Das* by Clinton B. Seely, Associated University Presses, 1990.

the true founder of modernism in Bengali poetry, and the presiding poet sovereign after Tagore.

In this regard, I always remember some graffiti I saw in one of Godard's films. The graffiti read: 'Poetry is a game in which the loser takes all.' Jibanananda's life seems to be a perfect example of this epigram. Likewise, I also remember the memorable words of Walter Benjamin regarding the life of Kafka: 'To do justice to the figure of Kafka in its purity and peculiar beauty, one must never lose sight of one thing: it is the purity and beauty of a failure ... One is tempted to say: once he was certain of eventual failure, everything worked out for him as in a dream.'

This amazing insight of Benjamin in envisioning 'the purity and beauty of a failure' in the fateful course of Kafka's life sheds an altogether new light on our idea of 'failure' itself. For one thing, both Kafka and Jibanananda created great art, in spite of severe failings in their personal lives. In other words, they did not fail in their works, they only failed in their lives. So we are faced with a paradox. Resisting the obvious temptation to utter the popular cliché that an artist has to suffer a lot to produce great art, how else do we try to resolve this paradox?

In my humble view, a part of this problem of failure lies in a crucial psychological factor of the artist's inner life. It's the factor of a robust creative solitude that an artist desperately needs to produce good art. This solitude serves as his creative workshop, his inner sanctum, his spiritual abode, which combines the characters of a temple and a castle. This solitude resonates with the meditation of a monk, the serenade of a lover, the kindness of a mother, and the anger of a revolutionary. It's therefore obvious that building up and buttressing this abode of creative solitude in an artist's mind is a matter of relentless struggle against the forces that drive our ordinary social lives. There comes the conflict between life and creativity. For me, this idea of creative solitude is of supreme importance in the nursery of art. Because I guess that this solitude is the extension of the solitude of nature itself that an artist acquires with much effort. It resembles the solitude of a forest in which endless forms of life are born at every instant.

An artist can acquire this mental solitude only through his intense and passionate contact with, and contemplation of, nature—the actual natural reality around him. The moment an artist loses touch with actual reality, he starts losing the power of his creativity. And here I must express my grave concern, though it may be a little out of context, about the dangers of digital invasion and distortion of our mind spaces by the internet and its social media. Excessive addiction to the digital, which operates on binary logic and propagates virtual unreality, is bound to cripple the creative faculties of man. Because it is plain to see that the binary logic of the computer is a deadly virus for the visionary magic of art. The creative mind of an artist is like the tender seed bed of a farmer, and exposing this mind to the prolonged onslaught of the digital is like suffocating the farmer's seed bed with plastic garbage. Risking the ridicule for sounding like a cave man in the age of computers, I would nonetheless appeal to all concerned to seriously think about this impending digital disaster threatening human creativity and find ways to combat it.

Having said that, I would now sign off by invoking the supreme image of an artist who epitomises this creative solitude that we are concerned with. It is the story of a trapeze artist written by Kafka shortly before his death in a sanatorium near Vienna in 1924, the same one that was included in his book *A Hunger Artist* which was published in Germany in the same year after his death. Let me quote an extract from the story:

> A trapeze artist—this art, practised high in the vaulted domes of the great variety theatres, is admittedly one of the most difficult humanity can achieve—had so arranged his life that, as long as he kept working in the same building, he never came down from his trapeze by night or day, at first only from a desire to perfect his skill, but later because custom was too strong for him. All his needs, very modest needs at that, were supplied by relays of attendants who watched from below and sent up and hauled down again in specially constructed containers whatever he required. This way of living caused no particular inconvenience to the theatrical people, except that, when other turns were on the stage, his being

still up aloft, which could not be dissembled, proved somewhat distracting, as also the fact that, although at such times he mostly kept very still, he drew a stray glance here and there from the public. Yet the management overlooked this, because he was an extraordinary and unique artist. And, of course, they recognized that this mode of life was no mere prank, and that only in this way could he really keep himself in constant practice and his art at the pitch of its perfection.[2]

As all of us are very familiar with Kafka's style of creating authentic allegories of the human condition in his works, we will easily recognise in the above passage not only his self-image projected in the image of the trapeze artist, but also his firm conviction about the compelling necessity for an artist to have an extremely ascetic and solitary life for the perfection of his art.

And yet, as I said earlier, in the digitally invaded privacies and sensibilities of our time, we are sure to dismiss this story as a mere literary construct coming from the almost psychopathic sensitivity of a writer, which has no bearing on the realities of our age. Thus we may smugly go about strolling in the high-vaulted shopping malls of art, glued to the smartphones in our hands.

But I, for my part, will continue to cast stray glances at the high vault of the mall, to see if the trapeze artist is really sitting there, on his invisible trapeze, very still and meditative, patiently waiting for the centuries to pass before he can start performing his high and sublime art all over again.

---

[2] 'First Sorrow', *Wedding Preparations in the Country and Other Stories* by Franz Kafka, Penguin Books, 1978.

Learning to Sing

Lydia Davis

You are in a neighbourhood singing group. You are singing with the others for recreation, for pleasure, not in order to perform. You enjoy it, but you are not satisfied with the way you sing. You would like to learn, at least, better control of your legato, your dynamics, your phrasing, and maybe, if you can, how to produce a better quality in your voice itself. You can read music quite easily, and you do sing on pitch, but your voice is thin and weak. One of the group suggests, after a while, that you might want to find a good singing teacher. She has a name for you.

You think it will be simple to learn to sing better. You will go to this good teacher, take lessons, and practise. She is in the next town to the north, the wife of a minister. She is very experienced and was once the coach, down in the city, to singers of opera. The lessons will take place in a room in the parsonage. You think that over time you can't help, then, but learn to sing better.

But it is not so simple. You discover during your very first lessons that the problem of singing better involves overcoming many other problems you had not ever imagined: to begin with, the problem of breathing, and the problem of how you stand—how you hold your body, how you hold your neck.

You try blowing on a candle. This is to teach you to control your breath. She has you blow steadily on the flame of a candle to see if you can make it flicker evenly. The weather is too hot to do this, it is the middle of summer, and it is, or feels like, the hottest summer you have ever experienced. But you do it. She has you expel all your breath before you inhale and sing. You should inhale as though you were sucking in the air through a straw. She asks you to watch yourself inhale in the mirror while holding your shoulders with your hands.

You are tense. You are so tense with yourself! she says. She asks you to turn your knees out and bounce, and to keep your knees slightly bent and flexible. Then she brings out a small trampoline and has you jump on it. She has you sing as you jump. This is supposed to loosen you up. She says, Yes, yes! She lends you the trampoline, you take it home, and jump up and down on it in the living room as you sing your scales.

You sing scales and practise the songs that she has assigned you. The first piece is an aria by Handel. It is a famous one, though you had not known it before. It is a beautiful aria that begins with the open syllable La, and the first notes are comfortably within your range. You are moved by it. But when you sing it, the sounds you make are not very pleasing to you. There on the page, as you read them, are notes that form a beautiful piece, but it is beyond your ability to create that beauty. It is your voice that is in the way. Your voice skips like the needle of a record. It squawks on some of the high notes. It is like something broken. She asks you to imagine that your voice, as it sings the melody, is a continuous golden thread.

Your teacher lends you a book on how to relax. But you are too impatient to try the exercises. You like to be active, and learning to relax is not active enough. Day after day you do not try them. You are aware of the book lying there in plain sight. Then you try one, and it seems to work. You make a good plan: you will do one exercise each day before you practise your singing. Now you begin to dread practising and you begin to avoid it. So you drop the relaxation exercises. Some days you are pleased, when singing at least a few notes, by the sound of your voice. On other days you are very distressed, feel your heart sink, and want to cry. The unpleasant sounds are so audible, so loud, so public, even in your own living room, in privacy, in your own ears.

Your teacher recommends that you try the Alexander Technique. You make an appointment to see the teacher of the Alexander

Technique, but she is very late for the appointment, too late for the lesson. You go again to see her. She says your spine has very good mobility, but that you should not consider your neck as separate from your spine. She discusses with you how you regard other people and how you regard yourself. You are so tense with yourself! says the teacher of the Alexander Technique. You are so tense with yourself! says the singing teacher again.

And why are you so critical? asks the singing teacher. Who was critical of you in your life? You think about it, but not for long. Of course, you know it was your mother. But it was your father, too—he did not disagree with your mother. It was also, sometimes, your older sister—though not your brother.

Your teacher assigns you a song by Schubert. You know the songs of Schubert very well, and many of them you like—they are satisfying in their harmonies and structures, though not moving to you. But you are holding your breath before you sing, and you shouldn't. You are taking a breath, a shallow breath, and holding it, and then singing. You should expel all the air first, take a deep breath and immediately sing, as if immediately rolling down the other side of a hill.

You are trying too hard, your teacher says. Who made you try so hard, in your life? You are assigned a song by Stefano Donaudy and then another song, one by Faure that you have never heard before. In fact, you did not know the songs of Fauré, only the *Requiem*, and they become a new love. They are more moving to you than the songs by Schubert. You listen to them over and over again, as sung by Véronique Gens.

Your throat is dry, so the teacher has you take a drink of water. You take sips of water, then you burp in the middle of a scale. You can't practise without sipping water, but you can't sip water without burping. Your teacher suggests that you drink more clear fluids throughout the day and eat fresh horseradish.

Then she suggests that you see a doctor to check your nose and throat, to make sure nothing is wrong with your throat, because sometimes your voice skips.

You make an appointment. You sing more songs by Fauré. You have not forgotten to think about your tension and why you are tense. But you have one small worry: if you cease to be tense, perhaps you can't go on doing the other things in your life the way you have always done them. Do you really want to change? Do you want to relax enough to be able to sing better, but lose the tension you need to do everything else? But perhaps that won't happen.

You hope the ear, nose and throat specialist will find something wrong, but not very wrong. It should be something simple enough for you to correct, so that then the quality of your voice will improve.

You sit in the specialist's office with a small camera up your nostril. A young resident watches your larynx and asks you to sing a note and then a higher note. The doctor who is training the young resident sings along with you. The voice problem turns out to be, possibly, not a voice problem but a stomach problem and you are given some pills to take, one each morning. You take one the next morning. Then, when you read more about the possible complications of continuing to take them, you put them away and never take another one.

The weeks are passing, and you are practising quite regularly. You practise in the living room, standing up, always when you are alone. If someone comes into the house, by chance, they are startled by your voice, so loud in the small house, and you stop. You may be improving, very slightly. What this actually means is that most of the time, you are singing in just the same way as always, your voice thin and weak, even tremulous, but that every now and then a few notes are round and full, though not yet rich.

Your teacher tells you that you must learn to sing from your chest, specifically from your breastbone. She tells you about what she calls *apoggia*, which, she says, means leaning into the sound.

She tells you to sing sitting down, to sit back on your spine. She has you sing sitting down, with the weight of your torso on your distal—though you don't know what that means. When the singing is better, she asks you, What did you do? But even when you like the sound you are making, it is thin, to your ears, which to you means young.

You think what is involved is also to sing more like a woman. Maybe you have been singing like a young girl. Maybe you are in fact more like a girl than a woman. You don't know exactly what you think you are. It could also be that you think you're a boy, but it is almost certainly not that you think you're a woman. It is hard for you not to feel like a young girl, anyway, standing in front of this teacher, who is larger than you and also seems older because she is a teacher, even though in fact she is younger, though only by a few months. In the first lessons, she kept saying how small you were, though you are not someone you would ever describe as small. You are almost sure, though you don't want to ask her, that singing better also involves being more womanly, or more like a woman. You wonder if it would help to be larger. Or at least to think of yourself as larger.

The teacher of the Alexander Technique, when you see her one more time, tells you to put two pillows under your T-shirt, one in front and one in back, and practise your singing that way. The singing teacher points to a buxom statue on her piano, in order to give you the idea. It is too hot to do that, you think, it is the middle of summer, and the hottest summer in many years. You do it anyway, but there is no change in the way you sing. You remark on this to your teacher. Your teacher laughs, because you expect everything to happen right away.

She asks, another time, if you are patient. Within certain limits, you can be.

You are trying to learn to stand up straight and keep your chin down, as she has instructed. You tell her this. But not too far down, she answers. On the other hand, you keep forgetting to let your voice 'drop' into your chest, into the area of your breastbone—that is, you keep forgetting about the apoggia, which, you remind yourself, means 'leaning in'. How does she have the wisdom, you wonder, not to comment until now that you should not be singing the triplets, three against two, quite so deliberately, so correctly? You don't understand how to fix that. Then you do think you see what she means, when you listen more carefully to Véronique Gens singing the first Fauré song. You wish, yet again, that your voice were good enough so that you could concentrate, with your teacher, on musical interpretation rather than on simply producing an acceptable sound.

After some months of this, on through the fall and winter and into the spring, it is time to prepare for a recital. You are not the only one who has been studying with your singing teacher. Most of her pupils are high school students—there is only one other older woman. Some of them sing well, and there is a tenor with a truly beautiful voice. Listening to him sing, you understand what it means to be moved almost to tears just by the quality of a voice. All of her pupils will take part in the recital. You are willing—you know it is a good thing to work towards a performance. Now there is more practising, and then there is rehearsing.

In the recital, you are to play the part of a lady attendant on the Queen of the Night, one of three attendants. That is all right with you. You like singing in harmony, which was why you joined the neighbourhood singing group in the first place. Each pupil, however, is also to sing a solo, and your teacher has asked you to sing the Handel aria that you learnt in your first lessons. You agree to do it, because you think that this, too, must be a good thing for your musical practice and also for your character, but you are nervous. She teaches you the small ornaments you should add when phrases are repeated, and she works out with you certain expressive hand gestures for you to use, though these seem to you rather artificial.

You would not be so nervous about simply singing the aria through accurately, from memory, if not very well. But, in addition to singing it from memory, there is another challenge. It has one rather high note that you must land on after the leap of a large interval. There is no way to make sure that you will be able to land on it successfully, without squawking. About half the time, practising at home alone, you don't squawk when you sing it, and about half the time you do. You can guess that you will be tenser than usual up on stage, in the church, in front of the assembled audience, even though they will be mostly families and friends of the young performers. You will be alone there, except for your teacher accompanying you at the piano nearby. You will be alone with a fifty-fifty chance of emitting an embarrassing squawk. Still, you are willing to try.

The recital takes place, and as it goes along, each pupil does well. The teacher has prepared them carefully. After the piece in which you play the part of the lady attendant, you change out of your costume and into your formal clothes and stand in the wings waiting for your turn to sing the aria. You are certainly nervous, but you expected that. Then you walk out, and you sing the aria. You don't forget any of it, though you come close to forgetting. You remember the hand gestures and the ornaments. When the moment comes for you to land on the high note, you do land on it without squawking, though not with a lovely sound, and you finish singing the aria, to your great relief. After the polite applause dies down, your teacher unexpectedly addresses the audience and lets them know that you began your lessons only the previous summer and have never before sung a solo on stage in public. She is proud of you, you know. The audience applauds politely again.

After the recital, there will be a break in your lessons, since summer has come again, the high school students are away, working at their summer jobs, and you, as well as the teacher, need to rest for a little while from the intensity of the practising and the rehearsals. A month or two later, you return to the parsonage, but now you are preparing to move away from the area, and when you do, that will be a natural end to your singing lessons. You are left with the knowledge that improving your singing ability would not be a simple matter, if you tried it again. You no longer have the illusion that by taking lessons and working diligently you could steadily improve your singing. Still, you may try again.

As for the recital, when you think back on it you still experience the same dread and nervousness, since there was never any guarantee that you would land gracefully on that note. It is true that you worked hard on the piece, and you did all you could, out there on the stage, to sing every note of the aria as you had been taught, but there was always an element of chance about your singing it successfully. You might just as well have made a dreadful squawk as you landed on the high note. That note would have been completely isolated in space, and in the attention of everyone listening, as isolated as any sound you had ever made, and it would have echoed through the vast spaces of the church, to your great embarrassment. That is why you continue to hear it in your imagination, and suffer it, though the recital is by now safely in the past.

There is a coda to this story. A few years after you move to the new place, you begin to take part occasionally in an instrumental group in which singing is optional—in other words, you may sing along to what you are playing, but you don't have to. Many people in the group don't sing because they are concentrating so hard on playing the correct chords on their instruments, most of the time bent over the frets. In the group, there is a very old woman, at least twenty years older than you. Her hands are gnarled from arthritis, so that she has to find inventive positions in which to hold and play her instrument. She is an enthusiastic and regular participant, though she usually leaves early, since she becomes tired. But it is her approach to singing that you notice. She does not have a good voice, and yet she readily volunteers to sing a favourite song to see if the group might want to learn it. You are told that she also sings in public, in front of an audience, when there is an open mic night. Her voice is thin, strained, scratchy. You don't know what to compare her high notes to—perhaps a scream of fright. But she is bold and unapologetic, with her head of curly white hair, her gleaming face, her bent back. She likes to sing these songs, and she knows a great many. And the group likes to hear her—it is her joy in the music that everyone appreciates, her good memory for lyrics, and her forceful character. You have never encountered this before—someone singing boldly and confidently with such a poor voice—and it is a surprise that gives you something to think about. You would still like to have a more pleasing voice, but you might be less afraid, now, of singing boldly and confidently, like the very old woman, with the voice that you have, such as it is.

One Door Closes, Another Door Shuts

Some Reflections on Failure

Tiffany Atkinson

Note: Soon after I received Amit's invitation to take part in the symposium, 'On Failing', I heard the slip of the tongue that prompted this piece, which became not so much a 'paper' as a series of creative-critical reflections on two failures, one personal and one public, that have happened recently (February 2020).

1. *One door closes, another door shuts*

I'm at a party trying to explain to a friend of a friend, i.e., a complete stranger, why I'll be spending Christmas alone. Somehow, I have slipped into this seasonal small-talk vortex.

But what about your family? he says.

Ah, well. In brief, I have one living and eccentric parent who has been married three times and woven for us both a complex web of familial estrangements. He doesn't 'do Christmas'. I am his only biological child and have no children of my own, which is to say that my efforts to become a parent, including a late and ill-advised effort at IVF treatment, have been slowly, repeatedly and expensively unsuccessful. Partly as a consequence of this my partner and I have separated. Most of my belongings are in storage while I renovate a hastily bought, tiny and much-neglected house, floorboard by floorboard, light-switch by light-switch. There is no working kitchen yet so inviting friends over is out of the question. And in any case, they will be busy with their own families.

Of course, I say none of this. I say, oh, it's a 'time of transition', with the little finger-quotes for ha-ha. Well, says the stranger amiably, raising his glass. Well, you know what they say. *One door closes, another door shuts!*

I smile. Wait.

Oh. No. Sorry! I mean ... He's flustered.

It's okay, I say, it's okay. And really, it is. His slip of the tongue, his unconscious failure to hold that second door open, hopefully, has not only put a new spin on the tired cliché of disappointment yielding unforeseen reward; it has furnished me with an unexpected moment of containment, an impasse, a framed failure that is almost restful in its domestic fatalism. For the moment, there is nowhere to go.

In my head an applause of doors claps shut back through the years, on all mine and my father's lost, exhausted, or otherwise failed partnerships, until the last one hangs ajar on a distant nativity: the radiant new mother, the recently promoted army officer, the infant, and our gentle spaniel Remus curled in the ersatz firelight of a 1970s Berlin army quarter. From a particular hetero-familial, upwardly mobile, middle-class vantage point, from the narcissistic point of view of nuclear family mythology, this was peak domestic and emotional attainment. Forty-odd years later, I am, genetically speaking, the end of the line. I have tried and failed to do my bit for genetic and sentimental posterity, but that door has closed, and (at last) I have heard the click. There is a moment of familiar existential panic, then for the first time since adolescence I allow myself to feel not stubbornly effortful, optimistic and resilient, but voluptuously, irresponsibly singular and doomed. A failure! There it is. I raise my own glass. *Cheers*!

2. If at first you don't succeed

Why bring this embarrassing personal matter into the context of a public talk? First, because I want to remind myself that failure, spoken of as something remote, speculative, conceptual, only distantly related to one's most intimate hopes and desires, is not felt as failure, not really—not once it has been helpfully curated into a triumphant or otherwise tolerable narrative of resilience. What I want to keep in mind is the affectively sticky, catastrophising, melodramatic, self-pitying, exceptionalising thickness of it, the shame, the obsessiveness, the blame, the powerlessness, the regret; because this is how I get to test what is at stake, what kind of conceptual apparatus is available to think about, to write about failure and failing, and to acknowledge the work involved in moving from its aggrieved self-absorption to a position that establishes some kind of fruitful engagement with the world.

It is also a caution about cliché, the cognitive trap into which we are apt to fall when using absolute terms like failure. In the dialectic of idiom, the opposite of failure must be success, no matter how circuitous: one door closes/another opens, and indeed we are obliged to keep banging on it until it does, since failure's condition must first be the effort put into trying. If you didn't want 'it' badly enough in the first place, you haven't failed so much as got what you deserved, and even if you've failed, you haven't really failed, you just haven't succeeded yet. You may yet get to cash your story of failure in for a story of triumph; this investment is exactly what keeps you in the game. It's a kind of affective Ponzi scheme.

This is one of the sustaining promises of meritocracy—and I can't help observing that IVF has much in common with neoliberal exceptionalism. The same layer of hubristic manifest destiny—'as a woman I deserve to be a mother'—held in place by murky empirical evidence and a hot core of emotional investment and magical thinking. *Just relax*, said the nurse during another barrage of invasive procedures, *that's the magic ingredient*! But statistically, IVF doesn't usually work. Statistically, one is not likely to be the happy exception, though one buys—both literally and figuratively—into the idea that the more rounds of the procedure you try, the more you are owed success. It didn't work for me, but in this respect, I am nothing special. This failure is sad, but it is not properly speaking a catastrophe or a crisis, which is a failure that is exceptional, utterly unforeseen. And between the door that closes and the door that shuts there is time and space, an anteroom of sorts, a poetic interlude, an impasse, where forward momentum, the narrative of the meaning of one's life, is momentarily suspended. In this space perhaps the feelings of failing can at least be detached from the pragmatics, and I am wondering what can happen there.

3. Be a good loser

To be fair, the Christmas party vibe was already heavily compromised by the UK general election on 12 December 2019, which, to the horror and despair of many, delivered the biggest Conservative majority since Margaret Thatcher's 1987 landslide. But then, it's not a good time to be to the left of anything, unless maybe you're in the Bullingdon Club and the port's coming round, which would be about 0.000009 of the UK population. The mood among the radical and centre-left, and all those who voted strategically in the hope of tempering the Tory majority was, and continues to be, one of despondency and recrimination. Certainly, it felt like more than a short-term electoral defeat: this result seemed to ring the death knell of left-wing ideology in the UK, exacerbated of course by the implications of Brexit and our now inevitable departure from the EU. If the Labour Party's heavy defeat was the second door to slam shut, the first was surely the Brexit referendum in June 2016, and perhaps also the thud of Trump's November 2016 victory, still reverberating brashly across the Atlantic. One door closes, another door shuts, and then yet another swings to. The question of electoral failure has become, for the left-leaning electorate, a national crisis, a failure that now feels exceptional and especially damaging.

What does it mean to be a good loser, a gracious failure, in a democratic context? I am not sure the UK can offer the best example. In the aftermath of the 2016 Brexit referendum, the forty-eight per cent who voted to remain in the EU were quickly dubbed 'Remoaners' by the 'Leavers', not least for the disbelief and outrage we expressed in marches, vigils and petitions, followed by repeated efforts to undermine the validity of the democratic process itself. A few Remainers in the Tory government at first sought to delay activation of Article 50, the process by which leaving the EU would be negotiated. Activist Gina Miller took the government to court in an ultimately unsuccessful attempt to have the referendum invalidated on the grounds it was unparliamentary. Multiple public petitions were made for a second referendum, in the hope that, given the right information, this would return the desired result. This approach was almost carried through into the Labour Party's electoral manifesto last year, while the Liberal Democrats' election policy promised to invoke Article 50 altogether and seamlessly if unfeasibly 'reverse' Brexit. Though I would have rejoiced myself had any of this proved possible, I have to concede that this behaviour, seen from the perspective of the statistical majority, is the hallmark of the poor loser, a sore combination of complacent privilege, hand-wringing and self-pity. To invoke the public-school sporting argot from which the gentlemanly notion of fair play and the good loser surely derives, the Remainer became the equivalent of the tennis player who smashes their racket or the footballer who curses the referee. No doubt the Brexit referendum was a disastrous embodiment of the adage 'ask a silly question', but had the Remainers won a majority of fifty-two per cent would we be calling for further referenda? It seems unlikely. We would surely have declared that to keep polling until you get the desired result makes a mockery of the democratic process, and is moreover a desperately conservative sort of revisionism. And, as the right-wing media consistently reminded us, 'the people had spoken'. We just didn't like what they had said. But that is democracy.

4. Winner takes all

There is an old joke that one cannot be a little bit pregnant, but after our IVF treatment cycles, I beg to differ. Reproductive technologies like IVF work not like the thunderclap of natural conception but by the slow accumulation of the odds of success. Their signals, so to speak, are more analogue—a continuous gradation—than the digital jump of binary data. For illustration: at our first appointment, my partner and I were given a three per cent chance of success, only they don't say 'success', they say a three per cent chance of 'a live birth'. This is before any intervention, any preparation, any labour, and highlights the attenuated, speculative process which involves, over months, intensive screening, the hyperstimulation of the ovaries, the harvesting of eggs and sperm, the insemination of eggs, the incubation of embryos, the implanting of them, and then the possibility of carrying a pregnancy to term. As each of these stages is passed the odds improve a little, so that by the time our embryos were implanted, we had boosted our chances of 'success' to a shimmering twelve per cent. Much like the pre-election opinion polls, each new statistic carries a magical aura. *Things are heading in the right direction. You are preparing to succeed.* No matter that the odds were ridiculous to begin with. We felt at each stage a little more pregnant, a little more 'winning at this', as buoyed up by the moral effort of trying, one door squeaks slowly open, then another ... This is the condition which the critic Lauren Berlant, in a different context, has called cruel optimism.

Cruel optimism describes the compromised relation that we, as individuals in a precarious neoliberal present, have in relation to the objects of our desire—this last a glib phrase that itself works to mystify the actual, material conditions of those hopes. Such objects arise among clusters of promises that make up eudaemonia, the classical notion of the good and meaningful life. Optimism per se, as a forward-facing attachment structure, is not in itself problematic. The compromise comes from the fact that the economic, political and social conditions that once facilitated an upwardly mobile good life as we currently understand it no longer exist. This is 'cruel' insofar as we are still unable to relinquish our attachment to the object even if we understand it to be impossible or damaging: 'A relation of cruel optimism exists when something you desire is actually an obstacle to your flourishing,' writes Berlant.[1] But in the end it is less the objects themselves, which on closer inspection usually reveal themselves to be flawed, than the deep fantasies they lay down in us that prove so hard to relinquish. 'Why do people stay attached to conventional

[1] Lauren Berlant, *Cruel Optimism* (Durham and London: Duke University Press, 2011), p. 2.

good-life fantasies—say, of enduring reciprocity in couples, families, political systems, institutions, markets and at work—when the evidence of their instability, fragility and dear cost abounds?' asks Berlant. Because of the sheer power of fantasy. 'Fantasy is the means by which people hoard idealising theories and tableaux about how they and the world "add up to something".'[2] And these fantasies are of course ideological. As Jack Halberstam puts it in his book *The Queer Art of Failure*, 'success in a heteronormative, capitalist society equates too easily to specific forms of reproductive maturity combined with wealth accumulation' or, more epigrammatically, 'success equals succession'.[3]

Thus, to keep trying despite the known likelihood of failure is to stay bound up in the compelling structuring fantasy; to let go is not just to relinquish the object, let's say the baby, but also to jettison the bathwater, the tub and indeed the whole rig of the house: the very apparatus that allows you to function as a person at all. It is not as simple as just finding another object to orientate yourself towards, since it feels pretty much as if there would be nothing left of you to point with. You need to build the whole apparatus again, claims Berlant, and at the same time dismantle the logic of success, says Halberstam. This perhaps is why failing hardly ever feels like a reasonable if unfortunate outcome, why it feels catastrophic. This is the situation that I think my partner and I found ourselves in.

5. It's the taking part that counts

What then of the fantasy structure of having been at least *a little bit pregnant*? Is there space for any meaning, any 'flourishing', in the partly attained object? Conventional success/failure logic would say not. But perhaps this is akin to the garish pie-chart diagrams that erupted across my social media the day after the general election, showing how, if in the UK we had proportional representation

[2] Berlant, *Cruel Optimism*.

[3] Jack Halberstam, *The Queer Art of Failure* (Durham and London: Duke University Press, 2011), p. 23.

instead of a first-past-the-post electoral system—an analogue rather than a digital signal—the Labour Party had not really done as badly as all that! The Labour Party and I are also-rans, casualties of cruel optimism, yes. But at least we were in the race, and we knew the terms of the competition and the promise of the good life we had bought into. As it happens, I found those pie charts oddly mobilising, though not in quite the intended way. They helped me to visualise a collaborative structure to trying, rather than a purely agonistic one where at the level of the individual, success is felt as a zero-sum game. They represent complex communities of people, and not just the metonymic individuals that come out on top. In putting these thoughts together, I realised there might be an analogous, if slightly embarrassing, pie chart for all of us who met awkwardly in the waiting room at the fertility clinic. The effect—and I am still trying to think this through so forgive the clumsiness—was somehow one of diffusion, or a lateral movement out of the self; as if, in the collective endeavour, some doors would open, and some would not, but the emotional cost could somehow be balanced out across the whole room so that the effort was not felt as a taking part in a solitary, agonistic battle against probability. In short, it was a feeling of internal pressure against the privatisation of failure. The structuring fantasy of the good life represented by the perfect little family is ideological, collective, after all, though like all things that appear to be 'common sense', it hides its workings well. And IVF is nothing if not intensely privatised, both as a financial and medico-legal institution and in the way that its shame and high personal stakes combine to make it a highly self-involved process for those who undergo it.

Since it is beyond my capacity to revolutionise the culture of fertility treatment centre waiting rooms right away, I will return to the UK general election, by way of Halberstam's work on queer failure, to explore what this 'internal pressure against the privatisation of failure' might mean in practice. On the morning after the election, alongside the social media pie charts, there was a flurry of postings from helplines and support groups, together with articles from leftist national newspapers, all of which recognised that the despair and despondency could have serious consequences for people's mental and physical health and for their ability to manage their lives. That it could be taken personally. It was not a call to engage in political debate, to keep trying to win that argument, but to turn sideways, as it were, and acknowledge the presence of the people next to you. For example, *The Guardian* ran an article called 'Don't Despair: a practical guide to making a difference: from food banks to fighting fake news', in which it advocated grassroots activism, community work and volunteering.[4] This was richly supplemented as the day went on by suggestions and links from readers. The article began:

> It's natural to feel hopeless today. A decade of deep cuts have already caused incredible pain, with growing poverty and crumbling services across the country. There are many people who will undoubtedly have woken up today and felt fear about the future. I have spoken to many over the past decade, from disabled people who have lost their disability benefits to those on low wages choosing between eating and heating.
>
> It is heartbreaking to think about what another five years of Conservative government will do to those who can't take a further squeeze.
>
> But there is always hope, just as there are steps we can take together. Charity is no substitute for a compassionate and competent state, and campaigning for political change will be the long-term goal. But in the meantime, it is a vital tool to help the poorest families get through – and to show we care.

I have never seen anything like this in a national newspaper in the UK. And I can't speak for evidence across the country, but I volunteer for a local food bank and by the end of that weekend the number of volunteers signed up to work at it had doubled. Yes, there is an element of do-good sentiment to this, but it is also

[4] Francis Ryan, https://www.theguardian.com/society/shortcuts/2019/dec/13/dont-despair-a-practical-guide-to-making-a-difference-from-food-banks-to-fighting-fake-news

legible as a claiming back of the agency of group relations outside of the political mainstream, or as Halberstam puts it, 'traditions of political action that, while not necessarily successful in the sense of becoming dominant, do offer models of contestation, rupture and discontinuity for the political present'. In this model, Halberstam argues, 'failure is the map of political paths not taken, though it does not chart a completely separate land; failure's byways are all the spaces in between the superhighways of capital'.[5] In these byways lies a space for building the motivational apparatus again, on different terms, while dismantling, or at least reframing, the logic of 'success'. The door on that neoliberal fantasy, which for the time being happens to be the door to 10 Downing Street, and the door of the White House, to name but two, has shut, closed, swung to. So, it may be helpful to think of the opposite of failure not as success, but as collaboration.

6. Fail again but fail better

This adage is the one that will be recognised as attributable to a renowned author, since it's a much-cited aphorism of Samuel Beckett, and one which happens to mirror 'one door closes, another door shuts' in its queering of the 'failure is just unrealised success' logic. So, I conclude with some speculations on how the space behind the shut door might have significance to writing practice. Since I am a creative writer, I would like to explore the forms through which failure might be refigured as significant without being yoked to a meritocratic narrative model of ultimate success.

Lauren Berlant, in *Cruel Optimism*, rather cryptically suggests that instead of constructing stories of triumph, one should 'become a poet of the episode, the elision, the ellipsis', presumably because traditional realist narrative genres are partly how bourgeois fantasy structures have come to pass for real life.[6] The elision and the ellipsis potentially forestall the headlong narrative rush through which plots deliver success as revelation or resolution. Certainly, experimental

[5] Halberstam, *The Queer Art of Failure*, p. 18.

[6] Berlant, *Cruel Optimism*, p. 34.

poetic writing already works as a challenge to the conventional reading practices through which one works towards a mastery of a text, a decisive interpretation, itself a form of hermeneutic victory. Elements of collaborative writing, collage, or the introduction of randomised composition methods like those used by John Cage, for example, might further limit the optimistic but misleading power of active intention and thus destabilise the notion of trying from the point of view of the poem as a piece of individual expression. Through this brief survey of structural premises, I felt the tiny flicker of a poem that might hold striving and failure in the same virtual space, but refuse to deliver an outcome because the poem doesn't know and has no interest in intention or interpretation. The poem would be a holding pattern. It would have the durational structure of an impasse, a productive kind of 'dithering', as Berlant puts it. Further, it would resist the easy but (to my mind) mendacious consolation that failure in any way makes one a stronger or a better person, even supposing I knew or cared to know what that might mean, or to whom. This poem would be a very small ambition indeed: or rather, its ambition would be somehow to sidestep the narrative structures of ambition. God knows, sometimes you just need to read something restful.

So I will finish by reading the first and only poem I have written around the IVF experience. This poem is a kind of holding pattern for cycles of trying, and the flashes of fantasy that animate them. Insofar as possible with a page-based format, it resists forward narrative momentum and could instead be read as cyclical in structure. Its substantial collage component comes from an old French lullaby, 'The Little Grey Hen', which has an obvious connection with how the intimacies of maternity are handed down from generation to generation, and which also brings in the rather embarrassing poetic/maternal register of babble. I hope this works to undermine the intentional, self-contained quality of 'voice' that often belongs to the lyric poem, and which certainly belongs to the many cruelly optimistic aphorisms we have built against failure.

La Poulette grise

an IVF lullaby

It's the grey chicken who lays in the church,
hunkering down where cold dust
hems her skirts
little sin-eater
She's going to lay a beautiful

It's the white chicken who lays in the branches,
lean as a whip of willow
in March breezes
little dream catcher
She's going to lay a beautiful
a beautiful little coco for

It's the black chicken who lays in the armoire,
freshening the rusty silks
for feast days
little pearl-warmer
She's going to lay a beautiful
a beautiful little coco for
her little one who's going to
do dodo

It's the green chicken who lays in the glazes
soft crystal tunnels
pecked by bees
little seed-hatcher
She's going to lay a beautiful
a beautiful little coco for
her little one who's going to
do dodo dodiche dodo

It's the brown chicken who lays in the moon
intuited egg of the tides
O sin-eater dream-catcher
pearl-warmer nut-warbler
seed-hatcher O
meteorite in the piazza
She's going to lay a beautiful
a beautiful little coco for
her little one who's going to
do dodo dodiche dodo. She's
going to lay a beautiful
a beautiful little

Some Spontaneous Reflections on Failure

Anurag Kashyap

This is the text of a brief talk given by Kashyap, followed by a conversation between the film-maker and Amit Chaudhuri.

Hi! I'm glad I made it.[1] I was told it would be cold in Delhi so I've worn many layers.

Failure has played a key role in my life. My life has been a series of glorious failures and somehow put together it's seen as a big success. I'll start at the beginning. I wanted to make movies so I started with theatre in Delhi, with Jana Natya Manch. I remember my first big show. I went up on stage at Prithvi Theatre where we were performing. I was so prepared to make an impression. I walked in and there's Shashi Kapoor sitting right in front of me—and I forgot my lines. My very first play, my very first scene, and I forgot my lines entirely. The other actors kind of cued in, they saved the scene and nobody ever found out that I had to say something. It started there.

I always took pride in doing things very well. I started my career as a theatre actor. I did two plays back-to-back and they were very big successes at Prithvi. I thought: I've made it! I had started getting acting offers in movies.

[1] Editor's note: Kashyap's journey to Delhi had been in doubt because of political turbulence in Delhi at the time, related to the anti-CAA protests, the film-maker's sympathies for the protestors, and concerns for personal safety that were allayed somewhat by the Aam Aadmi Party's success—rather than failure—in the Delhi Legislative Assembly election of 8 February 2020.

I signed up with some four–five movies and started acting. Then, I realised how limited I was with a different medium. Cinema is a very different medium as compared to theatre. I was in the hands of the film-maker, the director. I made some incredibly bad acting choices. They were such embarrassing movies that you will never find them anywhere; I made sure that they're buried.

In one of my movies, my co-actor was Imtiaz Ali. He also decided never to act again. The two of us decided we'd go and do something else. Imtiaz moved on to television and I started writing. The whole exercise of writing at that time, in 1993, was governed by film families, film families that had been controlling the industry for generations. We were the outsiders, and the first thing I realised was that as long as you don't pose a threat to them, they will let you in. I would go to them and say: I'll do anything, for free, without any credit. I was doing a lot of ghost-writing. I was learning the craft at the expense of someone else.

Then my first movie came out, which was a massive first movie where I was credited as a writer. It was kind of path-breaking and was a big turnround. I was very young to have handled that kind of success. That movie was *Satya*. After that, I decided that maybe I can direct, I am ready, with or without a lot of experience. This was also the time when I was young and very arrogant and also very determined. My whole idea was to disrupt the system, we'd do things our own way. I made my first movie, *Paanch*, and I went around saying, 'I'll find everyone who's never done a movie before', because I was an outsider, nobody gave me a chance. So all my actors were first-timers, all the crew were first-timers. We collected a whole lot of people and made a film that, in 2000, we thought was a very path-breaking movie. We were basking in the glory of this movie that we had made. But the censor board didn't know how to deal with it, and they also did not want to deal with these young kids with backpacks who were walking into the censor board room trying to teach them cinema.

Nobody wanted to listen to us and the film didn't release. So we started doing shows of the movie across the city, we did as many as 200 shows. We also showed *Paanch* at the CineFan in Delhi. We had so many shows, and every show people would come and we had so many pats on our backs and people would say: 'Oh, what a great film-maker you are.' I remember Boney Kapoor, who was a very big film producer, walked up to me and said, 'Anurag, I don't like you travelling in rickshaws and walking around with that backpack. You tell me which penthouse from Bandra to Andheri you want, and I'll get that for you—make a film for me.'

In my head I was thinking: 'My film has not yet come out yet and he's offering me a penthouse, what if my film comes out ...' So I said, 'No.' I turned him down. I kept waiting for my moment of glory to arrive and it never arrived. It never came. I was like, okay, fine, I'll make another film. I started working as a writer on *Black Friday. Aaj Tak*[2] had just come in and it had commissioned *Black Friday* as a six-episode series, as a study. When I wrote it, it was so controversial, *Aaj Tak* backed out. They said it's so political we can't do it. *Mid-Day*[3] was producing it, now they wanted to shelve it, and I started crying. I thought, no, this has to happen; how can this happen; which television will fund it; which television will show it; nobody will show it. Let's make it as a movie. The only person who stood by me was Tariq Ansari[4] and Tariq said: 'But we don't have enough money.' I said, 'Whatever money you have, I'll make it.'

So, from the writer I graduated to being the director of the film. We figured out ways to shoot this film. We wore documentary badges; we shot across the country. We had a large crew and we had no money, so we'd sleep in buses and then go and shoot. That's how I'd drive the whole team and we made *Black Friday.* When *Black Friday* came out, I thought *Paanch* will release at some point. *Paanch* followed by *Black Friday,* there's no looking back.

Black Friday got banned too. I was sitting dressed up—got my suit stitched for my first premiere—I'm sitting in the room and the phone call comes: the premiere has been cancelled because the court has put a stay order on the film. That was the first time it hit me very

---

[2] A television news channel.

[3] An afternoon daily published in Bombay.

[4] Managing Director of *Mid-Day.*

hard. I didn't get out of the room for the next two months. That was the first time that I went into thinking, why is this happening?

That's when you realise, you start looking into the mirror, and you realise that you're too cocksure about everything, too naive. You don't understand the way everything functions and you need to keep at it. After *Black Friday* got banned and two months later I came out of the room, I decided I will not wait. *What were you waiting for?* I was waiting for the glory, the accolades, everything. I started writing. That was the period when I wrote some of the worst films because I was writing just for money. I would do anything. I could write a hundred pages in a day, so anybody [who] last moment wanted to get a script done would come to me. I would just give it to them in three days and take whatever money they would give me.

I was trying to figure out what to do. In that period, in that moment of cynicism, I wrote *No Smoking*. It was very personal. I was very influenced by Kafka. I was very influenced by a whole lot of literature that I was reading. I decided I'll make a very personal movie about me in the system and be very intelligent. There's a whole metaphor of smoking which is around creativity and there's a man who doesn't want you to smoke and how he cuts off your fingers. In my head I had so many permutations and combinations of how it is.

I convinced my friend who advised me to go mainstream that I'm going to use your name in the film as the guy who keeps suggesting to me that I must quit smoking and that was Abbas Tyrewala. While we were making the film there was a running joke: we want to watch the faces of the audience. We should put up a camera on the audience and look at their faces while they're watching the film. We thought we were just these crazy, young geniuses who were making this film and people were going to be blown by it.

The film premiered at Rome Film Festival and there was this moment, we were watching the movie, I had Sean Penn sitting next to me and I thought this is my moment. I've arrived. Then again, when the movie came out, it didn't last one week in cinemas. It was the most trashed movie by the critics, it was a box office failure, it was everything.

It was all collecting together, all of these films, not working, not realising, getting stuck. For the first time, I wrote a film in anger. You want a love story? I'll give you a love story! You want songs? I'll give you a *Chitrahaar*. I got a music director and got him to do a series of songs. We did an album of eighteen songs. The film was made purely in anger to say okay, this is what you want, then this is what you deserve. You want mediocrity, I'll give you my mediocrity. It became my biggest success. It was *Dev D*.

Dev D was written purely in anger. I will subvert every goddamn thing and I'll give it to you in the garb of lots of songs.

It totally confused me. You want to do things in a certain way and that doesn't work. You invest so much in it, you invest yourself in it, and it doesn't work. That was also the time we started a blog. It was called *Passion for Cinema* [*PFC*]. That blog came out of, literally, totally, not understanding the changing world. I discovered the internet. I bought my first laptop.

The first thing you do when you buy a laptop and you go on the internet is: you Google yourself. So I Googled myself and I came upon a conversation on a site that people were having about me. Everybody had misinformation about me. Like a Santa Claus, I went into that conversation and I said this is me! And [that] this is not correct. [That] this is right. That was *PFC*.

They started talking to me and they said, 'Why don't you write?' I was very frustrated with the film industry and had a lot of anger. I started blogging and letting it out. Initially, my blogs were just me sitting with my whisky and with my one finger. Without full stop, without a comma, no grammar, nothing—I would just pour out everything.

It started to resonate with a lot of film-makers across the country. [For] Indian film-makers from across the seven seas, suddenly, that blog became much more than what we envisioned it to be. That's where Dibakar Banerjee came in. That's where Anand Gandhi came in, Chaitanya Tamhane, Vasan Bala, Neeraj Ghaywan. Every film-maker that matters today.

Someone was doing marketing; someone was in the ad-film industry. They came together on that blog. We started to reflect on how we would change the system. Everything we tried in the beginning, it worked. We decided to champion Abhay Deol, so we started signing Abhay Deol. Every film-maker on that blog made his first film with Abhay Deol and we championed how great he is.

We started to champion other film-makers. We were working like a mafia, a creative mafia. We wanted our kind of cinema to thrive, to flourish. By 2009, it happened. *Dev D* became a success. *Oye Lucky! Lucky Oye!*, *Khosla ka Ghosla* came out, Navdeep's film came out. Abhay Deol was a star. Everything started to happen.

That's when we lost our marbles. When you start to believe that: we have done this! Then everyone on the blog started fighting. Everyone wanted control. People wanted to buy that blog. The guy who was running it, who just started off on an impulse in 2006, suddenly was being offered money. He wanted to sell it. We wanted to keep it alive. It was a whole struggle. It went crazy. Everyone went in different directions.

The same thing that we had built up in our innocence and anger, when we became aware of it, it collapsed. That was the time I started a company called AKFPL. My first company, where we were trying to make the kind of movies we wanted to make. The whole idea was that because we didn't have money, we'll create a space, a kind of collective where we have a running kitchen. You can use the space in any which way, you can put your mattress and sleep there. You can use the edit room; you can work from that space. We'll collect money and we'll make movies.

The first movie we made was *Udaan*. *Udaan* became the first film from India to go to Cannes after many years. Then *That Girl in the Yellow Boots* went to Venice. In 2012, we had three movies at the Cannes Film Festival. In 2013, we had five films at the Cannes Film Festival from one small office. One of them was *The Lunchbox*. The way that *The Lunchbox* became so successful, it went to everyone's head. Except the film-maker who made it. Suddenly, *The Lunchbox* had many champions except the film-maker, who quietly went on to make other films.

I was trying to hold this whole thing together and I realised how we want to do things we're passionate [about], but when success comes in, in a way that we don't expect, we're not equipped to handle it. That's when we start making formulas, this is how it happened, we start calculating and measuring it and try to repeat it. But it doesn't create that same magic because it doesn't have that kind of spontaneity or honesty or truth to it.

I saw everyone falling apart. As the world took notice of us, we were already falling apart, AKPFL was falling apart. Everyone wanted to own a *Lunchbox* or a *Wasseypur.* I was never good with the business or the finance part of it so I always had to depend on somebody else. People were constantly trying to own things so much. In that failure, there was nowhere to go to.

From there on, I spoke to my friends and I said, 'Let's start another company.' We started collecting directors. We should make a company of people who are already making movies. That's when Phantom came in. AKFPL shut down and gave way to Phantom. Phantom was a director-driven film-making company. Phantom was seen as the outsider, the challenger to the mainstream studios. We started small with *Lootera, Hasee Toh Phasee* and then came *Queen. Queen* became such a massive success that none of us could handle it. Finally Phantom became a party place. Everybody started to party. Then we began to make these bigger budget films.

I was supposed to make *Bombay Velvet* which was my dream project. I had been working with Gyan Prakash closely for nine years, from the time *Black Friday* was banned and he invited me to Princeton to show *Black Friday.* From 2005-2006, Gyan and I were working on *Bombay Velvet.* The film was before the book came out. Gyan got tired and said I'm going to put out the book. So, I travelled across wherever the Portuguese went because I knew I couldn't get money to make the film so I figured out how to make the film at very less cost. But post all the success, the studios were giving us any amount of money we wanted.

My first instinct was to cast a very unknown actor for the film. Who I wanted to make the film with was a guy called Ranveer Singh. And then, everybody said Ranbir Kapoor wants to do your film, why do you want Ranveer Singh? So everybody convinced me, and said, 'We'll give you so much more money', and we are making a new company and we are getting a budget of 18 million dollars from FOX to make a movie that I was ready to make in 15–20 crores. And we fell for it. We fell for it. When you've spent that kind of money, you have to show that kind of money. I changed my complete grain of how I make movies.

I went against my grain. I literally thrive in chaos. When nobody knows what is going on I know exactly what is going on. And suddenly I was on a set where everybody knew what was going on except me. There were sets being made. We were living in a resort. We were travelling in a Mercedes to the set. And we were making this movie on a massive set we built up in Sri Lanka. And the film just somehow did not have that kind of a soul. It was because it just became so mechanical. And we were just so focused on the money, and the whole marketing and release was focused on recovering that money. That was the time when I went to one of my mentors in New York who helped me put the film together finally, and he's a big Hollywood director.

He said, 'Listen, the bigger the budget, the more democratic the edit room can become and in the edit room, as a creative person you need to be kind of in charge, you need to be dictatorial in that space. You have to be alone and you can't do that.' And from *Bombay Velvet* we came to *Shaandaar* and it just kind of started collapsing. People didn't know how to handle it. There were #MeToo allegations. There were lots of things that were going wrong in the office and we didn't know how to handle it. We were blind to it. Again everything fell apart. It fell apart and there was such a depression that hit me at that time, that, you know, nothing kind of ever comes together.

You're best friends and suddenly you don't talk to each other. 'I did not know he would turn out like this.' You start looking at your own role in it. How, with your silence, though it's got nothing to do with me, you become an enabler. You go through introspection and then decide: Do I need to form another company? Will I form another company? You give up. And the idea was, no, listen, I want to make movies. I want to make movies, and I can't stop making movies.

Luckily for me, Netflix came in at that time. We all went our own ways and formed our own companies and then Vikram[5] and I decided we'll work with our own companies together. *Sacred Games* happened. *Sacred Games* brought us back into that space, you know—that creatively we matter. And then *Lust Stories* happened. Success of *Lust Stories* was followed by *Ghost Stories.* Success of *Sacred Games* Season 1 was followed by the failure of *Sacred Games* Season 2.

Every time something happens—it happens everywhere. It's all pervasive, even a Netflix gets super excited. There are no checks and balances. Because everybody starts looking at it like—these guys can't fail. Actors, they have their doubts, they won't say it. Writers want to say something, they won't say it.

Suddenly you're staying in an echo chamber where everybody's telling you that it's great, it's fantastic. There are no checks and balances. You just go in, and you start doing things. Then the fall comes. That's how it has always been. It has always been like that. You step back and you keep looking at it and you learn from everything.

I've realised that every time you succeed, it's always followed by failure. Success always comes when you are not working for success. And failure always comes when you're working for success. It alternates itself. It alternates itself because there's always a learning. And it alternates itself only because there is learning. But we don't know how long the learning lasts. The learning lasts till the next success, and then again we kind of forget it. Then you again make the same mistakes.

Somewhere in the whole process you are trying to hold on to that one thread of your truth, and you're like you know what, this is it. Every time you fail, you realise that this is not what I wanted to do, and you try to hold on to that thread, and you try to communicate it, and then it keeps on happening.

Over the years, what I've realised ... twenty-seven years now ... I've seen more failures than successes, but those failures are far closer to me than the successes. Failure has always brought me back. Failure has always taught me so much more. I've failed in my

---

[5] Vikram Chandra, novelist, author of *Sacred Games.*

personal relationships, in my friendships, I've failed so many times, as a partner, as a father. But all those failures, when you actually acknowledge them, and it's important to acknowledge them, and dwell on them, they make you better.

Failure has always made me better, it has always brought me back, it has always given me a new drive. It keeps me going. One other thing that I have learnt all these years is: I very unashamedly talk about my failures. When you put it out there, even your slightest of vulnerabilities and admitting to those things, it somehow just keeps you going. It keeps you going because there's this tiny need of acceptance that drives you. You want your idea, your movie, or something to resonate with some person, somewhere. Like today, if somebody walks up to me and says 'I love *No Smoking*', I get very emotional. I want to stand there and talk to that person for a little while. But if somebody comes up to me and says 'I loved *Gangs of Wasseypur*', I say, 'Yaar, listen, let's move on from over there.' That's what it is.

Amit Chaudhuri (AC): The first question has to do with the Oscars, and Hollywood and the kind of subterranean or not-so-subterranean desire that you see playing itself out in people who talk about Hindi movies and some Hindi film-makers as well.

Anurag Kashyap (AK): Yes, we have a very unnatural obsession with the Oscars.

AC: That somehow the Oscars and Hollywood are a benchmark of some kind, and that if we conquer them then we will be there. While I feel that a great deal of substantial, really interesting things have happened in Hindi cinema and Hollywood has struggled, often, to make films of interest. That's one question for you to reflect on.

The second is on the creative process. To do with ... so you make a film and you don't know that what you're going to make is going to succeed. That's not what you're striving for. And then it succeeds, and with the next film you kind of lose your way—that resonates with me. That would resonate with many people involved with the creative process. That wanting to succeed or wanting to create something that is by other's estimation something that is an important thing generally leads to a failure in terms of the imagination. So is there a way of preparing to make something on your own terms?

AK: I'll answer your second question first. I was sitting with Gregory Roberts before his sequel to *Shantaram* came out. I was tied in with *Shantaram*, to work on it. I never liked the script. I said that it lends itself to a great series if you want to tell the whole story. But when you put it down into a movie—and he was so excited about *Magic Mountain*. He said this is the perfect sequel to it and the build-up he gave me of the book that without reading the book I sold the idea to Warners and said to combine the two and make it a series. Then the book came out and he disappeared. He left Bombay. He stopped responding.

It was eight years of build-up post *Shantaram*. *Shantaram* came out of somewhere very spontaneously. What happens is, when I make a movie, I work backwards. I know I'm making a film that's very personal. I go to my producer and I say, 'I want to make this movie entirely on my own terms. You tell me how much money you'll give me to make it if I don't tell you who's in it and I will not tell you what the script is. How much do you think you can recover.' They give me really small amounts and I work really hard on it.

I work backwards. I have to make this movie, it can't look low budget. I break it down and write a script with total fearlessness, my politics will be out there. Everything is out there. I don't hold back at all. I work with actors I like, I work with new actors. I can take many chances. I can go and pick up a new guy like Vicky Kaushal or a Sobhita because they have it in them.

I am totally fearless there. But, when it works, when it succeeds, it's not that you ask them to stop questioning you: they just stop questioning you. They give you much more money. Suddenly, there's a whole team that works with you. The team works with you because they believe in what you're doing. They'll work with you regardless. Suddenly you feel, last time nobody got paid very well. This time everyone must get paid. Then everyone starts getting paid.

Then, to justify we probably need a star, [we think] 'It's okay, we'll make them act.' Things start changing, the dynamics start changing.

The moment the star walks in, the politics goes out first. Everyone wants to play safe.

The moment studios walk in, the film can't be political anymore, the film has to be universal. It can't even be adult. Even sexuality has to be addressed in a way that it can be consumed very easily, like street food. Everything ... religion can't play a role. The big no's are religion, sexuality and politics. Then it gets out of hand, it doesn't stay your film.

Somehow the first people to reject it are the people who watch your movies for the very same reason, for a part of you. When a part of you is not in there, it starts to fail. That's what happens with success. When something succeeds, people start looking at you as a new voice. Or they'll say, 'He's back in form and he'll do something again.' And then they start giving you everything that you want. That's what happened when we made *Lust Stories*. Nobody knew what would happen, and it became such a massive success. We got twice the amount of *Lust Stories* to make *Ghost Stories*. And nobody questioned ...

AC: It's interesting that you go through this struggle because there are certain writers or artists who create early works which are extremely liberated and free and they are rewarded for that and then they are quite content to be constrained and successful.

AK: Yeah, because you know, it becomes a cycle. You want to keep on working. I can probably never make a *Black Friday* now. Right now, I'm in a process where I'm trying to find who I was. Because I've got material like that. So now I'm working on *Maximum City* with Suketu[6] and everyone. Because I know there's material like that. I need to find who I was. But do I really know who I was? I did not know who I was then. The idea is to not kind of corrupt it, the idea is to not poison it with anything external or try to be safe.

AC: So you have that artistic instinct which is almost like idealism, which some artists have but then give up at some point.

---

[6] Suketu Mehta, author of *Maximum City*.

AK: You don't give it up but are very unaware of when it slips out. Because you're so caught up in managing other external things, you lose sight of the very grain where it started from. For me, the biggest failure of *Bombay Velvet* is, the film came from a need to recreate a city in over four films. One film was fifties, one was sixties, one was seventies and one was kind of in-between.

Those four stories were the story of—one was the story of Raman Raghav—which was supposed to follow *Bombay Velvet* so I changed it and made it modern because after the failure nobody wanted to give me money to make it. One was the story of Nanavati, and there was another fourth story which was the story of Lloyd's Bank Robbery. So there were four films built around that. And the idea was to recreate the four stories, through the battle between Karakan–Karanjia, and how a lot of things were defined in that period and how they were documented.

Bombay Velvet was supposed to be a film about how the land was reclaimed from the sea. And the irony of it is that it's called Nariman Point, after a man who was the only man who protested against the reclamation. That was the film.

It became a love story. The politics went out. And we shot everything. We have all the footage we shot. We shot the whole reclamation, we shot everything. It was sacrificed. For the sake of the larger goal of recovering the 18 million dollars invested in the film.

The biggest sacrifice of the film was—they do these screenings to understand the audience feedback, and the audience feedback was, 'We see Ranbir Kapoor and Anushka Sharma too late in the film.' The children grow up fifty minutes into the film. So, twenty-five minutes of their childhood gets cut out, which is the actual history of what leads to this. So it becomes jumpy.

You look back and realise the mistakes you made and why you made those mistakes. But at that time, I was just handling my producers, my studios, everybody around me and trying to make the film less ... boring, because it had information and a whole lot of other things. What I forgot was, that's what they all read and came on board.

That's exactly what everybody wanted to make. Or was it that after the success of *Gangs of Wasseypur*, everybody just said yes to it and decided not to read it? I think the thing was, I was not cheating anyone. I only ended up cheating myself because I lost sight. I was only handling the current situation rather than going back and seeing where I started from. I think it slips out—somewhere it slips out in the heat of things. There was so much press on that film. It was the first time I was making a film with a studio, a big mainstream movie.

AC: Any comments on the Oscars and Hollywood or do you want to open it up to the audience?

AK: We have a very unnatural obsession with Hollywood. It's like how a lot of regional cinema looks for validation from Hindi cinema, we look for validation from the West, we look for validation from the Oscars, Oscars are not very different from Filmfare Awards. I am an Academy member, I vote for the Oscars. [With] the same Oscars—if the voting happened in December—*1917* would have won the best film. Because it was fresh and everyone was talking about it. One month later, in retrospect, everybody started feeling the film doesn't stay with you. So *Parasite* hua.[7]

A lot of things also go with the times. There's a lot that happens. Some of the greatest film-makers have never won an Oscar. Hitchcock has never won an Oscar, Scorsese won an Oscar for his weak film. I think some of the stronger writers have not won an Oscar. Say, for example, if you compare *Roger Rabbit* with a *Little Women*, what she's done with *Little Women*, I feel [it] should have won it.

There are a lot of other things that are at play. It's a lot of campaigning. It's a lot of lobbying. And a whole lot of things happen. In India, we feel that somebody has gone there and been nominated. They just go crazy. Without understanding the process of it. They don't understand that there are some very basic rules there. So, a film that doesn't have local distribution in the US, from a local distributor, will never qualify in the final five.

[7] So *Parasite* got it (the Academy Award for Best International Feature Film of the Year).

Like for a movie that goes to festival, people treat it as some kind of an Olympics, [but] it's not, it's a market. If you don't have a local sales agent or distribution, because all the festivals are funded by cultural bodies. If the local people are not benefiting from it, they won't select the film. It doesn't matter how good it is. Either it's got to have distribution in France or sales in France. If it's going to Berlin then in Germany.

AC: In Anglophone literature we have an interesting correspondence with the Booker Prize, but we won't go into that right now ...

The Intimacy of Failing

Amit Chaudhuri

Everyone I asked to participate in this symposium responded with delight to the theme, saying they knew all about failing first-hand. For instance, the poet Anne Carson's soft reply—I mentioned the symposium when we began talking on a walk back from an event to the hotel—was characteristic: 'I've had a lot of practice at that.'

Each response was also a confession of intimacy, made with a pride that was the antithesis of the kind symptomatic of social climbing. In India, we usually claim to know those who are already significant; we call them 'dear friends' and, if we are academics, cite them in the Acknowledgements pages of our books. Educated Indians have no 'dear friends' who are obscure.

Acknowledging failure, though—on the evidence of the reactions I had—gives us joy, liberating us from the rules of who and what and how to acknowledge. We reserve a special affection for failing, in a way we don't for the friends or colleagues we're proud to know. Many of my respondents smiled or laughed when I first mentioned the topic, as if failing was an aberration or a gift exhibited in childhood, which the world had now forgotten about. The laughter was tender, not acerbic.

It's easy to be attached to failing in a way that it isn't to success. Success is what we pay lip service to; with failing, we each have a distinct, enduring relationship. We can joke about it, as we can't about success, riffing on exhausted variants of the same punchline: versions of 'I'm sorry I will *fail* to attend your symposium because I already have a commitment at the time' came to me from several directions, as did, in my head, the thought, 'This time, I have *failed* to bring to the symposium many of the speakers I wanted to.' One doesn't joke about success in this silly way because we don't own it; success rules over us from a distance. Failure is ours; it will never desert us.

A memory comes back to me from 2011. Some Indian writers in English had gathered in New York for an event called the 'China–India Dialogues'. The authors' room was a nondescript space sequestered by curtains, and at one point I found the novelist Allan Sealy sitting there by himself, so absorbed in the booklet he had in his hands that he didn't notice me. 'What are you reading, Allan?' I asked; he looked up as if from a trance and showed me pages containing the bio notes of the authors. Given that these were, by prior directive, to be no longer than 200 words, they each had an identifiable shape, as sonnets or haikus do. 'Perfect lives ... such perfect lives ...' he said, as if responding to the beauty of each composition, including his own offering, and mine. A bio note must distil the essential successes. The notes that depart from this model and share little information are also paying it obeisance. We perform the bit of our achievements that we choose to, and keep to ourselves the knowledge that—as Orwell said when reviewing Dali's autobiography—'[a] man who gives a good account of himself is probably lying, since any life when viewed from the inside is simply a series of defeats.'

I got to know failure, and failures, early on, but I wasn't aware I had, because these weren't the terms in which such lives and people were presented to me. I have in mind my maternal uncles. Each comprised a model to be avoided; an inheritance to ponder. I viewed them from a vantage point provided to me by my father, a vantage point threatened and energised whenever it came into contact with my uncles. My father both belonged to and didn't belong to this family, the faux aristocratic Nandi Majumdars. He had known them—in Sylhet—since he was a child; he was the best friend of the second youngest of the brothers, the wayward, gifted Radhesh. The fact that my father was an only child and his mother had died when he was seven years old meant he was always in and out of my mother's family home. My father was intelligent, and it was either he or Radhesh who topped the class in school. But, unlike Radhesh—this narrative was implicit in the stories my parents told me, and vigorously underlined by my uncle—he was not a genius, and his progress, as a result, was more consistent in comparison to Radhesh's. In other words, common-or-garden success was to be my father's lot. There was a romance, an ideological position, to these stories, which instructed me that not everyone can be a failure.

My father—setting aside his life as a husband and a parent—had two phases in his existence. The first involved his startling trajectory from Sylhet to Calcutta to London to a job in Bombay to subsequent positions as Finance Director and then the first Indian Chief Executive of Britannia Biscuits. He was a beautiful, modest man, and some thought he'd prospered for his beauty and sweetness of nature alone. The second had to do with his wife-like relationship with Radhesh (who remained single all his life), and the latter's fits of brilliance and attempts to frustrate his own endeavours. Behind every successful man there may well be a woman; alongside failures, too, there's a steadfast companion. The companion rescues and salvages, but also protects failing's pristine qualities, having at some point noted their importance. The companion may lack singularity but has the ability to spot it in another. My father's relationship to Radhesh was a one-sided one of nurture. Radhesh's father, a civil engineer, had died from falling off his Australian horse when Radhesh was three years old. This led to a lapse in status in my mother's family, and to the dominion of idiosyncrasy. My father, by contrast, merely came from a landowning family.

Radhesh, deemed by my father and his own brothers to be, academically, the most outstanding boy in his school, invariably found obstacles in the path of study. One emerged from his fear of catching the august-sounding 'VD', or 'venereal disease'. He was convinced he could get it from any source, including urinals and even the pages of textbooks. My father found he was hardly able to turn the pages. His grades plunged. My father advised him but also shielded him from censure, waiting for the phase to play itself out. My father may have had conventional long-term goals, but he had unconventional long-term ones when it came to Radhesh.

Radhesh once asked his chemistry teacher on the street, 'Sir, how well do I need to know my chemistry text to do well at the exam?' The teacher remarked, 'You should know every word in it twice over.' My uncle—who could be a literalist when he chose to be—embarked on this project straightaway, but didn't complete it in time to take the chemistry paper.

In college, while doing what was then called the 'intermediate'—the stage before the BA—Radhesh was concerned with chemistry again, and, feeling he hadn't prepared enough, asked his teacher if he could repeat a year. Family lore says that the teacher asked him to get out of the room. Radhesh gave up on university at this point—a glitch whose significance may have been glossed over in the distraction of Partition. The family moved from Sylhet to Shillong. Here, Radhesh became a car broker, a conduit between buyers and sellers. My father had, meanwhile, gone to Scottish Church College in Calcutta, got himself a 'star' in his BA degree, with a 'letter' in English Literature; then he'd changed course—the equivalent of law conversion today—and gone to England to do Chartered Accountancy. Six years later, he was joined in London by Radhesh's younger sister, my mother, whom he'd proposed to in 1949 before leaving the country and then seemingly forgotten. Once my parents were married, they decided they must rescue the wastrel from car brokering and bring him to England. In England, Radhesh decided to take the impossibly difficult Chartered Shipbrokers' exams. The exaggeratedly lucrative domain of shipping was generally proscribed to non-whites and anyone who hadn't been to a public school. Radhesh stood first in England and the Commonwealth in the exam. My parents returned to India in 1961. Radhesh joined Phillips Brothers, the biggest shipping firm in what's known as 'the City'. He lived in a bedsit, sent money to other brothers in Shillong, urinated in bottles at night, and spent a lot of time at office, well after midnight, doing his juniors' work. When my father became CEO, he revealed to him that he'd been offered a directorship at Phillips Brothers which he'd turned down because it would involve too much travel.

Of the other brothers, three come to mind. Radhesh's Mejda, the second oldest: the story of him daydreaming when he was meant to be preparing for his BA. From a distance, it seemed he was inscribing something in the textbook. When his mother went near him, she found he was painstakingly writing, in ornate letters, the words 'J.P. Nandi BA'. She hit his hand so hard with a ruler that she fractured his thumb. J.P. Nandi passed his BA and then became a businessman. Finally, he became a mystic who listened to devotional songs all day on his gramophone.

Radhesh's Chhorda, the brother he was immediately junior to, was a man of great erudition, culture and literary talent. He became famous in Sylhet when a poem of his appeared in *Desh*, Bengal's leading literary weekly, when he was fifteen years old. He shone at university and then became a private tutor. He decided to appear for the Indian Administrative Service exams: everyone agreed there could be few better candidates in Shillong. One of the questions that year was 'Translate the national anthem into English'. Chhorda couldn't remember the words. Naturally, he failed. He took the Assam Administrative Service exam later and became Additional Deputy District Commissioner in Shillong. Taking no bribes, he was poor after he retired. He was one of those Radhesh sent money to and fulminated about in his isolation.

The youngest of the siblings was called Dukhu—from the Bengali word 'dukkho', or 'sorrow'—because he was born after his father died. There was nothing sorrowful about him; he was impetuous, and sang beautifully.

Dukhu became a mechanical engineer, trained in Germany, returned to Calcutta, and joined a leading German firm. Then, just as he was going to be promoted and transferred to Delhi, he resigned and started a business in agriculture-related machinery designed by him, because he could neither abide being in someone else's employ nor countenance being deprived (as he would have been in Delhi) of Gariahat Market's fish. His friends wanted to be partners in the firm, and he accommodated them until, my aunt says, his own position in it was no longer reliable. The machines he made were excellent but the marketing was dreadful. Among his contributions was the name he gave the company, Crushmore Maxban, the first word's rightness being self-evident, the second word the miraculous product, via the letter x, of a marriage between 'Ma' from Majumdar and 'ban' from Bani, the name of a partner's wife. Dukhu had no head for business. The feasts and helpings of goat's meat curry in the factory at Howrah on Vishwakarma Puja became epic through repetition. One of the oversize nephews, Kutu, would accept third and fourth servings, encouraging others: '*Khao, khao, compuny boro ase*'—dialect for 'Eat freely, it's a big company'.

Dukhu is the only remaining sibling of four brothers, one half-brother and two sisters. We visited him the other day; he's ninety-two. His wife reviews his decision to give up his job as if it happened yesterday. She's transported to the aftermath. So am I, though I have no memory of it. I would have been two at the time; but it's like a poem I can read and memorise and never fully understand—it has that capacity for surprise. She reveals a detail I never knew about the last days of her husband's employment: 'At night, I'd wake up to see him frowning and drawing diagrams. He was designing those machines.' Then, abandoning the reverie, she sighs: 'Anyway, it's done now.'

Of course, I viewed this past and its continuation into the present through the safety of the world my father had created in Bombay—the flat on Malabar Hill; the company car with chauffeur; the stretch between Little Gibbs Road and Nariman Point and Apollo Bunder. Although I didn't think of my father as successful, I knew, from these living examples, that there was a life outside success in relation to which the nuclear-family home on Malabar Hill, loving and deeply comfortable as it was, was constricted. My father, as he ascended, knew it too, which is why neither Sylhet nor my uncles' idiosyncrasies ever became invalid for him; they remained as infuriating and persuasive as they'd been when he first encountered them. 'They were the kind of people,' he said of the brothers, 'who would spend the entire morning arguing about which was the superior fruit, the mango or the orange, or who was the greater singer, Sachin Deb Burman or Vishmadev Chatterjee, and they would come to blows in the end.' We would shake our heads, as people do at accounts of fabulous animals that have unwittingly ensured their own demise and vanished from the earth; but there was also a warmth to our bewilderment, because of this grotesquely exaggerated surrender to what we deemed unimportant, and the neglect of what I in school was being told, repeatedly but without real conviction, was valuable. My uncles, as well as Sylhet and then Calcutta, where the youngest brother lived, became for me part of an education linked to desire: not to be what I was expected to be, but to allow myself to find out why it was crucial to decide between the mango and orange.

With this arose the question: why was there no scheme, earthly or divine, for this compulsive search for value? With this, before long, arose a seeming non sequitur: why was there no consensus about, or reward for, the truly excellent? One sees now why the debate about the mango and the orange was so freighted, and I understand in retrospect why my uncle in Calcutta so took it to heart when I said I didn't care for katla fish.

Education has to do with what you want to become, or where or who you want to be. What you want to become is not a blueprint; it's what you feel in moments of absorption. It has less to do with the ambition to go somewhere than with a desire that takes you out of yourself. So Cézanne painting the Montagne Sainte-Victoire is already physically present at the scene; but it's only in the paintings that the desire to be present is manifest, and is palpable. It's a longing that has nothing to do with reaching the destination or being there.

As I began to discover the unrewarded nature of excellence or achievement, I began to experience, while growing up, an absorption in the subject of the discovery—that is, in the unrecognised one—that was a variant of intimacy: not just to understand why the person was unrecognised, but to become, in the moment of bafflement, who they were. One such subject of repeated reverie was my mother: how could a singer of such originality and purity of tone not be famous? Record after record came out, but she was like a mythical creature inaudible to passers-by. First I investigated the question; then I immersed myself in it. My music teacher, Govind Prasad Jaipurwale, one of the great virtuosos of his generation, who died when he was forty-four; his father, Laxman Prasad Jaipurwale, the greatest creator of khayal compositions of his time, and an extraordinary singer—why are these names not on everyone's lips? At some point, I give up on disappointment. Confronting failing allows me to enter a state of absorption.

Gradually, inevitably, a family comes into being. Only I know its members. Many of them are dead. I make a catalogue. I'm transfixed by William Gedney. The beauty of his photographs is as difficult to pinpoint as are the reasons for Gedney's obscurity in his lifetime. As I turn from photograph to photograph, I find it impossible to separate the singularity of the images from the resistance beauty has to becoming immediately visible. In this sense, an artist's reputation, or the place of excellence in the world, is as inexplicable as a human being's future. I find it difficult to demarcate the intimacy I feel with the nature of Walter Benjamin's work from the curious immersion I experience when thinking of his decision, upon returning from the French–Spanish border, where he was told his papers were inadequate, to take opium and end his life. He actually had the necessary papers, and would have gone through with other refugees the next day. I hoard this detail.

Underneath my father's accommodation of my mother's brothers must have been the knowledge that acting in the right way, thinking and saying the right thing, precludes access to not only a significant domain of experience, but to truth. His background—the only child of a landowner; the son of a mother who died by suicide when he was seven—may or may not explain his kind of patience, just as it may or may not account for his journey towards becoming the CEO of a 'multinational' company in Bombay. But the tolerance of idiosyncrasy—which is basically a term for the inculcation of self-impediment—is very different from the liberal, multicultural or Constitutional tolerance of a multiplicity of world-views or religions. It's to accept an aberration from the correct way of thinking, from the proper life, in the interests of what one might call, in the absence of a more intelligible phrase, spiritual veracity. It's a way of responding to the world that we've forgotten alongside our forgetting of the many histories of failing.

Thinking back now, I realise that my uncles prepared me for certain tonalities and contradictions in literature, for its curiously antithetical relationship to likeability. The curmudgeonly and its companionship with new registers of meaning; Philip Larkin and his poems, especially 'Mr Bleaney' and 'Dockery and Son'—I wonder in what way I would have received them if I hadn't known Radhesh? Here is the narrator of 'Dockery and Son', thinking back to his school acquaintance as he sums up his life in a moment of wakefulness:

> But Dockery, good Lord,
> Anyone up today must have been born
> In '43, when I was twenty-one.
> If he was younger, did he get this son
> At nineteen, twenty? Was he that withdrawn
>
> High-collared public-schoolboy, sharing rooms
> With Cartwright who was killed? Well, it just shows
> How much ... How little ... Yawning, I suppose
> I fell asleep, waking at the fumes
> And furnace-glares of Sheffield, where I changed,

And ate an awful pie, and walked along
The platform to its end to see the ranged
Joining and parting lines reflect a strong

Unhindered moon. To have no son, no wife,
No house or land still seemed quite natural.
Only a numbness registered the shock
Of finding out how much had gone of life,
How widely from the others. Dockery, now:
Only nineteen, he must have taken stock
Of what he wanted, and been capable
Of ... No, that's not the difference: rather, how

Convinced he was he should be added to!
Why did he think adding meant increase?
To me it was dilution. Where do these
Innate assumptions come from? Not from what
We think truest, or most want to do:
Those warp tight-shut, like doors. They're more a style
Our lives bring with them: habit for a while,
Suddenly they harden into all we've got

And how we got it; looked back on, they rear
Like sand-clouds, thick and close, embodying
For Dockery a son, for me nothing,
Nothing with all a son's harsh patronage.

I know that Radhesh too exhorted his married friends and relations that 'adding ... was dilution'; though I'm not sure that what he'd engendered, in the end, was 'nothing,/ Nothing with all a son's harsh patronage'. 'Nothing' is a complex and underrated idea. Whether the narrator of 'Dockery and Son' represents a feasible model for existence, whether he's wrong or right, is beside the point. What's instructive is the means by which many of us can be persuaded to keep such a person's company: or our inexplicable friendship with Larkin's casual, less-than-palliative tone. In my final year at University College London, I recognised the persuasiveness of not only an inappropriate style of living but of a resistant language and wrote a dissertation on Larkin called 'Lyrical Elements in an Anti-lyrical Voice'. As far as I recall, I don't think I argued that one was a vehicle for the other, but that they both subsisted in the same ecology. The only human being I was in regular contact then was Radhesh. This may have had something to do with a word I used earlier: 'education'.

I'm creating these possibly specious contiguities more than three and a half decades later; but I was very aware, by the time I began my DPhil on the poetry of D.H. Lawrence, of my uncles' contribution to my cultural temper. I had become interested specifically in Lawrence's unevenness, his—in the eyes of his critics—inconsistency, his ability to be, according to them, both a great and a bad writer, to fulfil and betray expectations, to lapse from the extraordinary to the intolerable. I was intrigued also by the nature of my interest; by the low threshold exhibited by contemporaries such as T.S. Eliot when confronted with unevenness of style or thought; by my own comparative calm, and willingness to embrace Lawrence in his entirety, rather than just make room for his most fully realised poems and fictions, echoing the calm I felt in the face of Radhesh's various forms of hectoring in London, and my father's patience when it came to his friend. Here is Eliot, reviewing John Middleton Murry's study of Lawrence, and offering his own assessment of the author:

> Lawrence was not a 'pure artist', in that he never succeeded in making a work of art ... He had plenty of sensations, undoubtedly; no man of his time was more sensitive; but he could neither leave his sensations alone and accept them simply as they came, nor could he generalise them correctly.

Sometimes my father and I had approached Eliot's position when it came to Radhesh; yet we shared a conviction, without ever expressing it to each other openly, of the validity of disorganisation: of difficulty—not in the sense that Eliot would have understood it, as a mastery of craft, but as a lapse in the sensible, and as a life-giving interdependency between excellence and idiocy—being a tenable working model. 'But to me,' Eliot continues, '[his achievements] indicate that Lawrence ought to have been a "pure artist", but was impure. And I wonder also whether, had Lawrence been a success in this sense instead of a failure, Mr Murry would have been so interested in him.' I wasn't struck by Lawrence's failure, because I didn't think of him as one. This is because of a background in which my uncles had come to me not only as the sum-total of their lives, but as excess: this had given me the capacity not so much to have an insight into but to understand—as you might say 'I understand' when considering the errant actions of one you're intimate with—Lawrence's language.

It would be wrong to say that, having grown up in a desultory, aimless world, I find myself living, since the 1990s, in an age of success—that is, in a time to which success is all-important. We live in an age of survival. Success is no longer the fruit of achievement. It's the difference between existence and obliteration. Consequently, the successful and the unsuccessful are both marked by desperation.

I sensed this from 1991 onwards, two years after the Berlin Wall came down and Communism ended, when my first novel was published. I knew already that I had embarked on an eccentric trajectory; that what I'd chosen to write wasn't in keeping with the boom in Indian writing in English or in the novel in general. Yet I reaped some of the benefits of that boom, under false pretences, until I realised—not for reasons of morality, but in the interests of whatever was creative in me—that I must protect myself from it. At the end of the last millennium, I fled England for Calcutta. For a while, I abandoned the novel. I played with the extent to which I could approach unpublishability. In the early 2000s, I concluded that I must continue to publish in order to write unpublishable works.

From stupidity, the inability to make peace with things, arises the work. There's no good time now to send the work out into the world; on publication day, you feel the opposite of belatedness—you pray the book is treated well, but regret its publication, because you're convinced it deserves something better. Writing books is not at all like having children and sending them out into the world.

I'd started dreaming of ignoring success, till I came to terms with the dream's untenability. I can't fail purely, because my failure, then, will be paradoxically non-existent. In capitalism, only success has existence; there are no alternative, negative modes of subsistence. For my failure to exist now, I must invent ways of succeeding slightly. I test the temperature from moment to moment, because it's important to check the conditions that make this possible.

Failure

A User's Manual

Sunetra Gupta

Failure as a state in relation to success

When asked by Amit Chaudhuri to speak at this symposium, I thought it would be easy for me to put together a set of thoughts on my own extensive experiences of failure, ending perhaps on a celebratory note endorsing the various ways in which failure can actually be used to enrich one's life. But eventually I decided that I'd prefer to embark upon a Russell-Whitehead type of journey towards something that is pure failure, and not failure that is encumbered by some kind of relationship with success.

I am used to speaking about failure mostly in practical terms when I address audiences on topics such as women in science, or what it's like to be a scientist and an artist. In these public talks, I often bring up failure, but the kind of failure I refer to in these situations is not pure failure; instead, it may be thought of as the leeward side of success, the dry downward slope, the inevitable fall.

We've all experienced that inevitable fall after any kind of success, small or large. And sometimes it is not even a fall but a plateau, a stagnation that is captured with such extraordinary delicacy in Elizabeth Bishop's poem 'Crusoe in England':

> Now I live here, another island,
> that doesn't seem like one, but who decides?
> My blood was full of them; my brain

bred islands. But that archipelago
has petered out. I'm old.
I'm bored, too, drinking my real tea,
surrounded by uninteresting lumber.
The knife there on the shelf—
it reeked of meaning, like a crucifix.
It lived. How many years did I
beg it, implore it, not to break?
I knew each nick and scratch by heart,
the bluish blade, the broken tip,
the lines of wood-grain on the handle ...
Now it won't look at me at all.

Failure as an anti-climax to success is, of course, a common theme in literature. Tennyson's Ulysses laments *being stuck by this still hearth among these barren crags/ matched with an aged wife,* but also feels *'Tis is not too late to seek a newer world./ Push off, and sitting well in order smite/ the sounding furrows.* He does acknowledge *We are not now that strength which in the old days/ moved heaven and earth; that which we are, we are,* which does constitute a form of reconciliation with failure but also is perhaps closer, in some ways, to the notion of pure failure in being ultimately pathetic rather than heroic; nonetheless, it still contains that impurity of an urge to succeed and remains, therefore, a kind of failure that ultimately only comes to relief against the backdrop of success.

Have I experienced this kind of failure? Well, yes, I have—perhaps most spectacularly in my literary career, where I enjoyed a certain degree of security in the 1990s, publishing four novels with mainstream publishers, and winning a degree of literary 'acclaim' through the odd prize (or its long and short list) and lengthy reviews in the standard outlets. For a variety of reasons—having very young children, the difficult circumstances under which I gained a permanent position at the University of Oxford and the responsibilities that it came with—it took me over five years to write my fifth novel, *So Good in Black.* But by 2005, mainstream publishing was completely closed off to me. While this experience was rather unsettling, it did not constitute pure failure as it could be easily classified as the absence of success. That it led to many, more fulfilling, opportunities does not alter its position within the taxonomy of failure I am attempting to construct, although it does redeem it in other meaningful ways as I'll explain later.

Another kind of failure which one tends to trot out in public lectures is the kind which provides a springboard to success. I often illustrate this at a personal level with the resistance I have faced in my scientific career to new ideas I have proposed. I use mathematical models to try and understand how pathogens—the viruses, the bacteria, parasites that cause infectious disease—evolve and spread. There is a sort of linear narrative that's established in people's heads about how pathogen populations march relentlessly through time under the forces of natural selection; the theory that I have been consolidating over the last thirty years challenges this idea and effectively replaces it with a more nuanced non-linear narrative. My ideas have not been received with unalloyed enthusiasm from the scientific community. In particular, when I applied this theory to influenza, it was either directly derided or ignored. I responded to this by trying to test this theory through experimental methods, and this led my research group to identify a new way of making a universal flu vaccine that should be capable of protecting against all strains of influenza rather than just those that are currently circulating. We were able to patent this technology, and are now engaged with industrial partners to try and test it further. And the truth is, if people had believed me, they would have gone and done this themselves, and I wouldn't be here saying I'm making a universal flu vaccine. So that's a tangible example of how failure has created the conditions for me to embark upon a new and interesting journey, taking my theoretical findings into the clinic.

Failure as a process

So it is true that under certain circumstances, one can capitalise on failure and there is indeed a growing industry in instructing individuals on how to make the most out of failure. Much of this trades on the highly stochastic nature of success and, in effect, what it teaches (and for which there is a huge need) is resilience. I noticed on the London Underground, the other day, a prominent advertisement for a book entitled *How to Fail: Everything I've Learned from Things Going Wrong*. I got the strong sense that what was on offer were recipes for coming to terms with one's own imperfections. However, imperfection is much easier to overcome than failure. Failure is a gritty business.

While presenting failure as a route to success is very far from the notion of pure failure that I wish to explore in this essay, it does establish 'failure' as a process rather than a state of being; it also consecrates failure as a process of refinement and rebalancing rather than being simply about perseverance.

There are, in particular, certain pernicious elements of success to which failure can serve as an antidote or as a regular detox session to get you back on the rails. In this symposium, Anurag Kashyap referred to a sequence of glorious failures in his career which rescued him from the 'poison' of success. This is certainly a constructive use of repeated failure, but it is only available to those for whom success is generally within relatively easy reach; for these privileged few, the torque between success and failure can become a sustained and sustainable force.

Beckett's inducement to fail and then fail better would appear to adhere to this principle and even introduces a sort of forward movement in the dance between failure and success, but only if we subscribe to the notion that 'failing better' brings us closer to success. I would argue instead that what Beckett really meant by 'fail better' was to sink further and more deliciously into the state of pure failure—but more of that later.

Amit spoke about how the inability to fail is itself a kind of curse. That reminded me of why John Berger did not believe Picasso to be as important an artist as many of his contemporaries—Berger argued that Picasso existed within a static condition of success, that he perfected a style but then remained fossilised within it.

For Tagore, failure was an essential requirement for spiritual progress. His song *Aamare tumi ashesh korechho* (*You have made me endless, tipping me out over and over again, so that you may fill me with new life*) is shot through with a delicate humility regarding this enduring play between us and the universe. Even upon the death of his beloved son, Tagore was able to summon the strength to write:

> My light has been quenched upon this dark and lonely path
> For a storm is rising
> A storm is rising to befriend me
> Darkling disaster smiles at the edges of the sky
> Catastrophe wreaks delighted havoc with my garments, with my hair
> My lamp has blown out on this lonely road
> Who knows where I must wander now, in this dense dark
> But perhaps the thunder speaks of a new path
> One that will take me to a different dawn.

For him, the possibilities for replenishment contained within the human spirit were infinite.

Towards a definition of pure failure

But what if you reach a point where you can't be replenished? This surely is a state of pure—and ultimate—failure.

Such an event does not need to be the culmination of a recursive process between failure and success but may arrive in the form of catastrophe, as in *Oedipus Rex*. Already it suggests a use for itself in that the reduction of the individual to this condition is what allows them to fully claim the one thing that remains—which is human dignity. This is perhaps why Terry Eagleton has said that, in Athens, tragedy was a form of ethical political education for the city-state as a whole, not just 'a night out for the toffs'; there was even a state fund that the poor could use if they didn't have the means to pay for tickets to the theatre.

An essential element of this form of catastrophe (or 'peripeteia') is recognition (or 'anagnorisis')—in other words, a transition from ignorance to awareness. Dignity is acquired through knowledge, but there is no possibility of co-existing with this knowledge. The will to self-destruction, which Clancy spoke of with such candour, could therefore be interpreted as an extended urge to assert one's personal dignity—that it may occur in parallel with the small acts of self-care he mentioned suggests that the root cause is anything but self-disgust. Instead, one may see it as a manifestation of the Aristotelian principle of Thought in the construction of tragedy, whose language is civil discourse and rhetoric rather than despair.

That 'knowledge' and 'thought' may lead to such a state of pure failure (exalted though it might be) will not sit well with the purveyors of these 'commodities' who, within the current neoliberal order, now extend well beyond the writers of self-help books to encompass institutions of higher education—all seeking to guarantee success and inure you to the various (minor/impure) failures you might meet along the way. There's no place for pure failure within the free market, not just on the part of the writer but also on the part of the reader.

And it may be the case that 'pure failure' of the kind that I have identified here belongs to the temple rather than the market, so to speak. Much of what we treasure, we do not seek to sell. It is simply unfortunate that many such institutions which were once within the temple have now relocated to the market, leaving those of us who have a more complex relationship with failure (let alone 'pure failure') in the lurch.

Pure failure as a 'natural and viable' state

Having moved closer to a definition of 'pure failure', it now falls upon me to interrogate whether it is a 'natural and viable' state as Amit has described in his talk.

Pure failure is clearly a condition from which there is no guaranteed exit. As Tiffany Atkinson puts it: one door closes, another door shuts, and you're stuck. My User's Manual should then be concerned with how one endures this state of pure failure and maybe renders it into what one might call a productive state.

Rilke calls us 'wasters of sorrows'. He accuses us of not employing sorrow in the same way that we recruit happiness to enrich our lives. In fact, a closer examination of the two Tagore songs I've quoted earlier shows that the latter (*My light has been quenched ...*) is tonally much closer to a state of pure failure and presents, in many of its elements, a viable solution to living within pure failure; being escorted by disaster to a 'different dawn' is fundamentally different from being repeatedly filled with 'new life'. Tagore is secure in the latter, but much more provisional in entertaining the prospect of arriving at a location where the darkness within him will give way to a wholly unfamiliar burst of light.

An alternative to this essentially romantic approach to pure failure is afforded by irony; once again, it cannot shield you from the pain of pure failure but it can provide a state of productive tolerance through modes such as surrealism or, indeed, plain nonsense. My hero, in this regard, is Marcel Duchamp who embraced pure failure more richly than any other artist I know—giving it all up in his thirties to play chess for the rest of his life after having failed to enjoin his contemporaries to stop producing 'retinal art' (guaranteed to please the eye) and instead 'to put art back in the service of the mind'.

The New York Metropolitan Museum of Art presents him thus:

> *Subverting traditional or accepted modes of artistic production with irony and satire is a hallmark of Duchamp's legendary career ... Duchamp is associated with many artistic movements, from Cubism to Dada to Surrealism, and paved the way for later styles such as Pop (Andy Warhol), Minimalism (Robert Morris), and Conceptualism (Sol LeWitt). A prolific artist, his greatest contribution to the history of art lies in his ability to question, admonish, critique, and playfully ridicule existing norms in order to transcend the status quo—he effectively—sanctioned the role of the artist to do just that.*[1]

The energy of many of these movements ultimately derives from our fundamental inability to comprehend reality, even in physical terms: the inadequacies of representation (through the limited apparatus of our five senses) never being fully compensated by our more abstract efforts (will, etc.) to get closer to the thing in itself.

---

[1] https://www.metmuseum.org/toah/hd/duch/hd_duch.htm

With regard to fiction, I've spoken of how I exploit the gap that exists between the word and its referent, and how I exploit and enjoy the inadequacies of grammar, syntax, narrative, all of which constitute a fundamental sort of structural failure of language to represent reality. And this is also true in science, particularly of the language of mathematical modelling which is what I use to understand infectious disease systems. There is a misguided notion, even among those who claim to be experts in mathematical modelling, that models should strive to become more realistic. But it is actually precisely the avoidance of realism that gives models the power that allows us to gain insights into systems. Our fundamental failure to perfectly 'capture reality' lies at the heart of all scientific endeavour and this is something we should celebrate, because we have lived within that failure very successfully. We have written equations that have allowed us to send rockets to the moon, just an example of how well we have exploited the 'pure failure' of our inability to engage directly with the physical world.

Some exceedingly practical uses of pure failure

At a more mundane level, one can use 'pure failure' to permanently, rather than periodically (as in Anurag's case), liberate oneself from the constraints of success. Ranajit Das gave us a most delightful account of his very successful courtship of 'clandestine fame'. I like to think that my own experience in the literary industry has placed me in a similar situation: rejection by mainstream publishers has led me to independent publishers like Women Unlimited and Interlink Books, where I have the immense privilege of interacting with editors of the calibre of Ritu Menon and Pam Thompson. I have also been fortunate in finding a highly sympathetic literary agent in Esmond Harmsworth whose sophisticated and sincere responses to my first drafts have helped them find their ultimate shape.

The failure I suffered has also liberated me fundamentally as a writer and irrevocably altered my relationship with what I write. While it is true that I never did try to pursue a course that would put me in the literary limelight, to have not casually achieved this anyway has created even more of a breathing space for me to do exactly what I want when I address myself to the beloved task of writing. It's been years since I finished my sixth novel and it's only just doing the rounds with publishers. I've just started on a seventh and am looking forward to failing to finish it for as long as I like.

Another obvious pursuit of failure in my life was my decision to pursue two careers, which I have talked about in a previous Literary Activism symposium on Deprofessionalisation. I can't say I've completely failed in either of my careers, but it's certainly possible that I haven't achieved the success that I might have been able to if I had chosen to focus on just one of them. An American writer I very much admire in other respects said to me some years ago: 'You should do one thing and do it well.' And I thought about and came to the realisation that I don't do things in order to do them well. Obviously I want to perform to the best of my abilities, and gain some fulfilment in doing so, but that's not my primary motivation. I do what I do because I want to do it, and if that leads to failure—so be it. As Amit said: 'Success rules from a distance. Failure is ours, it will never desert us.'

Failing Light

Sumana Roy

Even though it might sound preposterous to blame poor light for being a failure, I'm not the first person to do so. The idiomatic, reinforced by centuries of disappointment with light, squats in this phrase: 'failing light'. I'm going to talk about the failure of light. One of the reasons is this—that at least light won't take it personally, while my fellow humans might. For what distinguishes light from humans in this regard primarily would be this—light has no sense of failure, or so I'd imagine. This provokes the most obvious question—is it possible to fail if one has no sense of failure? What might failure mean to plants and animals, and to the elements, for instance?

As I think back to my first sense of this question, carbon-dating my history of thinking as it were, I find myself with my father, he still young, very young, with a moustache, and muscles that needed to work all the time. A village boy who'd been changed by the encounter with cinema when he moved to Calcutta as a college student, he now wanted his little children to taste the same magic. We were in Siliguri, a small town—then even smaller, in the 1980s—in sub-Himalayan Bengal, where none of the films that had made him a convert were available. When the VCR arrived—by arrived I mean when it became affordable for middle-class families like ours—my father became a missionary. He thought of cinema as an aesthetic that was capable of reforming us, and he wanted to ensure his children didn't fail to respond to the medium with the naturalness he had when introduced to it. My brother and I were put on a regimen of Satyajit Ray and Ritwik Ghatak films, and, at my mother's insistence, occasionally

Mrinal Sen. My father's industriousness in acquiring copies of these films stuns me now—for there was only one 'video parlour' in Siliguri then, a tiny boxed room called Chhaya Chhobi. The word literally translates to 'shadow picture', a metaphor borrowed from light—it's the Bangla word for cinema.

One of the first films forced on my brother and me was *Kanchenjunga*. I later got to know that Baba had chosen this film simply for the familiarity of its title. In the Siliguri of the 1980s, one could not not be aware of the Kanchenjunga. It was just there—not like sand in a desert, but more like our mother's eyes, which we imagined following us everywhere we went, preventing us from doing many of the things we wanted to. On most mornings it was visible from our terrace; it was there when we cycled to school, even though the day's busyness seemed to move it farther away slightly; and it was still there in the afternoon when I followed my mother to the terrace to collect the clothes she'd hung to dry. Why would we have to watch a film about something we knew almost as closely as a relative?

Kanchenjunga would be the first time Satyajit Ray would make a film that wasn't based on another writer's material. It was meant to be set not in Darjeeling but in a 'bagan bari', a farmhouse, in the suburbs of Calcutta. If Ray had not changed the setting, it is possible that my father would not have chosen this film as part of his instructive curriculum for his children. The 'story' of the film wasn't new for us. We were used to relatives visiting Darjeeling to see the Kanchenjunga, and then stopping at our place in the foothills for a night before they took trains and buses to return to Calcutta and other parts of Bengal—the evening would be spent recording their disappointment with the mountain peak. They had, like the people in Ray's film, spent the entire day in expectation, moving from 'spot' to 'spot', hoping desperately for a moment's sighting of the reluctant peak—but they had met with no success. The word 'success' was theirs—they used it while speaking in Bangla, as if that would emphasise their failure.

Ray's genius, as we know, lies in turning this everyday event into a thriller—the suspense is built upon an axis of failure—set over the period of a day, in which a Bengali family consisting of an industrialist, his wife, their daughters, move around in Darjeeling, meet or run into people from Calcutta, having decided to end the day, which happens to be the last day of their holiday, by watching the sun set over Mount Kanchenjunga. The industrialist has two daughters, one of whom he is trying to get married to a man of his choice; a daughter's marriage is breaking down; the other daughter turns down her suitor; an unemployed young man is trying to get himself a job.

And yet, in spite of these human failings and failures, it is the failure of something else that is at the heart of the film: the failure of the Kanchenjunga to reveal itself to its seekers. We know that the mountains—in this case the Himalayas—are there, that they cannot move, and yet we're curious: what exactly is it that we seek to see? A kind of lottery that allows this sighting, a function of light and mist? What fails us therefore are not the mountains but light. Here is a nine-year-old Satyajit recollecting the same mountain peak—there's an intimation, here, of an aesthetic that would guide the film and, indeed, his career:

> I had been having a good time at Darjeeling ever since we arrived but one thing made me feel quite sad. It had been misty and hazy every day and I had not yet seen Kanchenjunga. My grandfather's painting of Kanchenjunga hung on a wall in our house in Calcutta. I was dying to see the real thing, to find out how it compared with the painting. At last, one day, while we were staying at Elgin Villa, my mother woke me very early in the morning. I ran and stood at the window. In the painting, my grandfather had caught the evening sun falling on the snow, to the left of Kanchenjunga. Now, I could see the sun's first rays falling on its right. I gaped open mouthed, and watched the faint pink glow turn to golden, and from golden to a shimmering silver. Later in life, I got the chance to watch many beautiful sights, both in my own country and abroad; but I do not think anything can match the beauty of Kanchenjunga during sunrise and sunset.

As in this recollection, the Kanchenjunga does eventually reveal itself at the very end in the film—but such is the human conditioning in failure that by then the Kanchenjunga has no watchers.

I see *Kanchenjunga* as an extension of Ray's cinematic study of failure, expressed metaphorically in the failure of light. When asked by the actor Soumitra Chatterjee why he had chosen cinema among all the art forms that interested him, Ray replied, 'Once, when I was a student at Santiniketan, we were taken to different parts of India to draw and paint. We even managed to visit the caves at Ajanta and Ellora. I realised that all these extraordinary works of art and literature had been created in India already. It seemed to me that there was no opportunity anymore to climb to the pinnacle of excellence in these fields. So I have chosen a medium of art in which there is room for fresh work. We haven't made much progress in cinema in our country. That is why I am a film-maker.'

Reading Satyajit Ray's essays and interviews, one cannot not be made aware of his acute awareness of failing, and how that awareness affects the choices he makes to avoid or compensate for what he, in various places, calls 'risks' and 'problems', and how those choices affect his films, primarily their aesthetic. 'When we began, there was a problem at the very outset,' writes Ray in the essay 'Two and a Half Years with Apu'. He could very well use this sentence for almost every film. Ray himself uses the equivalence between 'failing' and 'failing light' from time to time. Writing about a scene in *Pather Panchali*, his first film, he says: 'The next shot was going to show Sarbajaya throwing away the remaining rice on a heap of rubbish, and Bhulo (the dog) polishing it off. But this shot could not be taken on the same day that we took the previous ones. The light faded away, and so did money in our pockets. And with the money went the rains—nothing could be filmed during the monsoon.'

Here is Ray: 'On bright, sunny days in October, I began going to the village with Apu, Durga, other members of the unit and all the equipment, hoping fervently that it might rain. Even a small dark cloud in the sky made us gape, and wonder if it would, by some magic, spread all over and come pouring down. Finally, one day, our prayers were answered. The sky was covered by thick, black clouds and it started raining in torrents. Durga ran to join her brother under a tree, both looking for shelter and hugging each other. She chanted a rhyme under her breath in the hope that that would make it stop raining: *Nebu pata koromcha/ hey brishti, dhorey ja* (Lemon leaves, fruit and berries/ stop at once, what rain there is). ... It must be admitted that the scene turned out very well. Anyone who has seen the film, I think, would agree.'

This is part of a pattern. The script comes to be written, plans are made, and then upset. Circumstances, the aleatory character of life, puts together another plan. I feel moved by his pleasure in this unexpected result of failing. 'Unexpected' is a word that Ray uses often, when characterising the nature of failure—when is failure ever an expected thing, after all? In an essay called 'Project Tiger', he writes about the harassment he faced while shooting with a tiger.

> We were ready. The door of one of the cages was unfastened. Mr Thorat called out to the tiger. It responded almost at once and sprang out of its cage to land on the open space outside. What followed was totally unexpected. ... Instead of walking sedately in a dignified manner, the tiger started prancing around with tremendous enthusiasm. It leapt, it jumped, it rolled about, dragging its poor trainer, who was desperately clutching the wire tied to the tiger's collar in a futile attempt to bring it under control.

After all this, when a few shots are taken and Ray returns with his team to Calcutta, he realises that the 'camera had failed to work properly. The shots were too dark, so much so that the tiger was merging almost completely with the background of trees and leaves.' Ray's writing about his films, his recollections about them, is actually a record of a unique kind of anxiety, a premonition—though that might not be the word I am looking for—of failure that affects the implementation of the script and the eventual optical destiny of the film. I cannot help noticing this arc, in broken lines as it were, between what was to be, and, superimposed on it, what we eventually see on screen. That awareness of the gap between the script and the modifications forced by circumstances on it reminds me of the European modernist painters—painting over an old canvas without whitening its remains as it were. This is a record and an idiosyncratic optic of failing in Ray's work, if failure can have an optic at all.

Failure, we will agree, is a retrospective awareness, and this it shares with success—that it is always the dead frog on the dissection tray, that it can be analysed only as a function of the past. This we have all experienced, whether from moment to moment, in our imagined half-written obituaries or as athletes might, even, though rarely, in the middle. Failure is therefore like love—one is aware of it only after one has failed or fallen in love, not that I am equating the two, but then, who can tell. That is not the kind of failure that affects Ray's aesthetic—it is not located in the past tense but in the future: hence its unique, even idiosyncratic, relation with kalpana, the imagination.

After travelling for unending miles in search of a desert where they needed to shoot only a couple of scenes for *Goopy Gyne Bagha Byne*, Ray is exhausted. He writes: 'Every ten minutes, one of us asked the driver, "Where is the desert?" And each time he replied, "We'll find it."' A few paragraphs later, after many changes in what Ray calls 'scenery', he writes, 'We had travelled for twenty miles, and yet there was no sign of the desert. Was the entire trip going to be a complete waste? The money we had spent on petrol, the time we had spent, the bumps and jerks in the jeep we had suffered?' A little later: 'We had taken the wrong route right from the word go. The desert was in a different direction altogether.'

There is a fabular quality to these narrations, fables that seem to emphasise failing and failure as integral and unexpectedly empowering to the creative process. The desert, as imagined by him, both as scriptwriter and film-maker, could not be found. And? Ray writes: 'Very well, we agreed to set out once more. This time, only a mile later, I saw a place that—strictly speaking—was not a desert, but I knew I could not find a better place for the scene I had in mind. If this place had a name, we never learnt it. Here, there was plenty of sand, but not the wavy sand dunes one associates with a proper desert. The sand stretched tightly on a flat surface for as far as the eye could see ... The afternoon sun fell directly on this land, its light reflecting in the sand and dazzling our eyes. It was not particularly warm in late February, but when seen through our camera, I had no doubt that this stretch of sand would seem no different from the Sahara.'

'The rewards of failure' is a cliché—it is consoling and moralising at the same time, and yet it is one I find myself using when thinking of how it applies to a film-maker's work. This is, to repeat myself, a trait that belongs to the process, one that is, by its very nature, bound to remain invisible. The search—the quest, almost—for the desert, the promise of finding it, discovering a desert that is not quite a desert, and then the mirage that creates the illusion of a lake—I see this as a metaphorical understanding of what I call the rasa of failing.

'We reached the site for the shooting to find the actors and the remaining crew waiting anxiously. The only thing that had *failed* to wait for us was the sun.' (emphasis mine) This is a refrain in Ray, one where the literal transforms into the poetic, one that enables what is essentially deprivation to transform into surplus. 'Failing light'—or even 'fading light'; both are phrases that Ray uses—is a term that I have used to talk about not only the relationship that a film-maker or an artist has to light, but as a synecdoche for the possibilities that failing might open up. In one paragraph he complains, 'There was no way we could shoot this precious scene in the fading light.' In the next, he writes, 'One look at the sky told me that the postponement of our shooting was another blessing in disguise. The sky was now flecked with grey and white clouds. Golden sunlight, streaming through the gaps in the clouds fell on the desert, thereby giving us a light that was suitably striking for this dramatic scene.' Soon, something has gone wrong—there is no smoke coming out of the engine, a visual quote that Ray had imagined as integral to the scene, and so he despairs, 'We had to start all over again.' The man who had been in charge had been 'so busy watching the shooting that he had forgotten to put enough coal in the boiler. ... Okay, but this time we could not afford another mistake. The light was just right.' It seems to be a cycle, this pair of disappointment and delight, and they give a shape to the film—to any work of art—that is almost analogical to an artist working around a disability, whether biological or circumstantial.

It is akin to the painter Benode Behari Mukherjee, Ray's teacher at Santiniketan's Kala Bhavana, developing a way in which to paint after blindness had affected both his eyes. Ray made a short film on Mukherjee, and in a moving essay titled 'Benode-da', quotes from the painter's explanation of his 'failing'.

> What happens is that one develops a totally new concept of space. Space becomes a solid object, which has to be manually pushed aside in order to move forward. Nothing has any existence except what one can touch. You can see a chair and know that it is there; I will know that there is a chair only when I sit on in it. Even then, I won't know whether or not it has arms until my hand brushes against them. ... There is another side to it, you see. I picked up that glass full of tea. Until I became blind, I was never really aware of how glass felt to the touch. One develops tactile feelings about every object. ... But I've had problems. I cannot tell when I've run out of ink. I may be sketching happily when somebody says suddenly: Why, your pen's not leaving any mark on your paper! So now I've stopped. I've begun to lose interest in colours. I used to cut pieces of coloured paper and make collages, but now I've come to realise that it's impossible to verbally describe the exact shade of a colour. I've tried to explain it by saying it's blue like such-and-such an object, or it's red as such-and-such a flower, but there is always a doubt about its precision. What still interests me is form. And tension. ... That's the main thing.

The Inner Eye. The title of Ray's film about Mukherjee, but also more. What Ray is arguing for is a space for failing in the tradition of unpremeditated art—an art that is as accommodative as a paragraph, an art that is as accommodative as the human heart. In the essay 'Films in Colour', he writes about shooting *Kanchenjunga*.

> I am reminded here of my experiences while shooting *Kanchanjungha*. A Hindi film was also going to be shot in the same place, at the same time. Bearing in mind the weather conditions in November, provisions had been made in the script of *Kanchanjungha* to include cloud and mist as well as sunshine. The Hindi director was going to shoot a song sequence. In the

> twenty-six days that we took to finish shooting *Kanchanjungha*, we took every possible advantage of the swiftly changing natural conditions. In those twenty-six days, the director of the Hindi film failed to shoot even that one song sequence simply because he had to wait for the sun to come out.

Ray is, as you can see, making a case for the aesthetic of provisionality, of contingency, of an acceptance and consequent incorporation of the ad hoc nature of the elements and circumstances that affect the process of creativity. It is the nature of life to disappoint, and hence the natural gravitation towards an alternative, a negotiation with failing. This is from an essay called 'Two Problems':

> Those who paint may have to make do with poor quality painting material, if one day good quality paints and brushes become expensive and scarce. If they cannot get paints, they can use chalk, and even if that is unavailable, there are pens and pencils. I have seen Nandalal Bose draw with twigs from a neem tree (used normally as toothbrushes).

In another essay, 'Some Aspects of My Craft', Ray says this about 'designing':

> The designer has to work within the limits of these specifications. This is not necessarily a constricting factor, but it does impose on him a collaborative and interpretative function rather than an independent creative one.

In another essay, one whose title is again an annotation on failing, 'The Odds Against Us', he makes the same argument, about the enriching possibilities of 'problems', problems that one now takes to be the reason for failure.

> The studios in Calcutta show their hallowed past in every crevice on the wall, in every tatter on the canvas that covers the ceiling. Some of the families of rodents that inhabit the rafters have lived there ever since the foundation of the industry. The floor is pitted,

> the camera groans as it turns, the voltage begins to drop after sundown. The general air of shabbiness is unnerving. And yet I do not mind these at all. I do not think of these as hindrances. After all, we have the essentials to make a film, and it is within us to make it badly or well. It is the bareness of means that forces us to be economical and inventive, and prevents us from turning craftsmanship into an end in itself. And there is something about creating beauty in the circumstances of shoddiness and privation that is truly exciting. Yes, I am *happy* to be working where I am.

In an essay called 'Film Making', Ray, never a moralist, shares an anecdote that almost borders on the moral, about the real risks—and dangers—of being adamant about a premeditated idea of art. He is writing about—yes, yet again—the problems that he had to face while shooting *Jalsaghar* (*The Music Room*).

> The truck arrived in the evening. In the *failing light* I watched the crane being pushed along a couple of stout wooden planks on to the top of the truck. It seemed a risky operation. And then, before I realised what was happening, half way up the plank, the crane tottered for an instant and then crashed on the coolies, killing one instantly and crippling another for life. I stood rooted to the spot, barely ten feet away, stunned by the magnitude and suddenness of the tragedy. It took me some time to realise that all this would not have happened if I had not set my mind on those overhead shots.

Failing light. Stubbornness, as Ray reminds us, is costly—his insistence on the shooting going to his imagined aesthetic cost the coolie his life; it also—and this is not to make a comparison—costs artists their art. When I think of 'failing light', I think of Satyajit Ray and Benode Behari Mukherjee, and I also think of the Ajanta Caves and my father. I was nine, and was again being force-fed 'art' by my father—this time inside the caves. At first it was a relief to be inside them, a refuge from the festering heat that squats in these parts of India, refusing to leave for months. But I was a child, and children are, after its initial surprise and magic, bored by darkness. I knew little Hindi, but, after my father's most serious questions to the tourist guide, I asked him what was for me the most important question: why was it so dark here?

The guide's answer was a paraphrase of what he had just narrated to us—about the architecture of the caves, planned in a way so as to give the calm of darkness necessary to meditation for the Buddhist monks there. What illumined the caves was not sunlight but the luminescence of the frescoes—I remember thinking of them as the equivalent of lamp posts in my small town. Light fails even when it is tied to a lamp post—it is an animal on a leash. It cannot move beyond its penumbra. The analogy of the lamp post might have also been triggered by childhood memories of my father and neighbourhood uncles kicking aged trunks of lamp posts in annoyance and anger in 1980s Bengal, kicking them until some stroke of coincidence brought them to life after the forty-fifth kick or so, and we'd believe this to be a cure for power *failure*.

The Ajanta Caves were built between the second and fifth centuries BC. Their walls tell stories of the lives of the Buddha as much as of the daily lives of the people who painted them, citizens of unique, even experimental, early Indian states, of large groups of people in buildings and jungles, ponds and mountains. William Dalrymple mentions the colours that 'glow with a brilliant intensity: topaz-dark, lizard green, lotus-blue' and Yashodhara Dalmia their 'mesmerising synaesthetic wraparound quality ... which seem to loom towards the viewer'. In spite of efforts at restoration, because of the nature of the painting material used, and perhaps because of a history of the caves being flooded, a large body of work stands destroyed. When I think of the Ajanta paintings, it seems to me that it is almost as if they were coded to fail, a failure intrinsic to its life, to their incomparable aesthetic—I think of the fungi and the microbes and the phototactic insects that are attracted to the painting material that gives these paintings their luminosity, those that destroy them, and I think of the failing light inside the caves, what our tourist guide had called 'handicapped' art. The lack of light hadn't allowed completion—or completeness—the tall man had argued. Many years later, I would find myself thinking about this when reading the allegory of the cave in Plato's *Republic* and I would wonder what it was about failing and caves and light that they would keep returning to human history in cycles of metaphor.

You might be wondering why I have been talking about Ray's relationship with light through this prism of failure, or why I have been returning to the Ajanta Caves and my father, in asides, while talking about Ray. All of this has been to illustrate, to myself as much to you, that I think of 'failing' as a rasa. Rasa is, as you know, an aesthetic theory that goes back to fourth or fifth century CE in the Indian subcontinent—it means 'juice, taste, essence'. Originally there were eight rasas: bhayanak, fear; hasya, laughter; rudra, anger; adbhuta, wonder; bibhatsa, disgust; shringar, love, romance, attractiveness; veera, heroism; karuna, sadness, as we see in the *Natya Sastra*; santam, peace, was added to the list by Abhinavagupta in the tenth century CE. The theory of rasa is a theory of effect—emotions, or bhaavas, were 'produced' as a response to the text. The fear of failing, however, begins as an emotion in the artist. You may have noticed, therefore, that by arguing for a rasa that has a life before the birth of the text and not necessarily visible in its blood afterwards, I have dislocated the site of the rasa from effect to cause.

There is no rasa in the *Natya Sastra* that holds in it the sense of failing. Fear is horror, not the anxiety of failing. When it plays out in our emotional lives, it changes us in ways that we recognise only in retrospect—affecting the vocabulary of self-understanding the most. It changes the language in which we speak to ourselves. That language, that leads to and from a vocabulary of failing, is one that cannot be shared, not even with those with whom we've shared almost everything: spit and soul, sweat and passwords. The language of failing cannot be shared just as the rasas, and our unique experience of them, cannot be shared with anyone. 'Failing light' is a phrase that has solidified over time—it's a phrase that reminds us of the impossibility of calibrating failure and reiterates the inadequacy of the vocabulary of failure. It is perhaps because of this that it has fallen through the cracks of art and literature. It might also have to do with the stigma attached to the word 'failing', the near-criminal banishment of those who experience it in our society—one 'suffers' from failure, after all.

Turning to Ray and the Ajanta Caves and Benode Behari and my father, I am made aware of how a sense of failure might lead to creative empowerment, that the rasa to do with feeling like one might fail is *not* a negative bhaava but one capable of producing accidents denied to premeditated art. When Rabindranath Tagore says '*aaro aalo, aaro aalo*' in a song, asking for light, 'more light, more light', or when Kazi Nazrul Islam, his contemporary, in a devotional for the Goddess Kali, sings '*Kalo meyer payer tawlaye dekhey ja alor nachon ...*' ('Come, look at the light beneath the dark girl's feet ...'), one becomes aware, again and again, of the riches of failing, and of failing light.

Unlike the other rasas, whose nature it is to be manifest, the rasa of failing is meant to be invisible. If it were visible, the work of art would have failed. That is its peculiar nature. I also think that the sense of failing as a rasa has been amplified because of the times we live in. I have often wondered why Bharata, and Abhinavagupta after him, did not consider the sense of failing as a rasa. The answer would perhaps come from Abhinavagupta himself, who argues that, no matter what the emotions invoked, in a 'truly poetic composition', the 'ordinary pathological symptoms of emotion lose their significance ... and we have one enjoyment'. Joy, ananda. The inseparability of joy from failing. Ray and his teacher, my father and the anonymous painters of the Ajanta Caves, recognised that failing and ananda inhabit the same neighbourhood. These were people formed by a time before 'failure' became a new-age professionalised category. I think of a common gesture, or tic, signifying failure in Indian culture, a gesture that is an inheritance from an older time—the biting of one's tongue. I think of that as the mudra—the gesture—for failing. After all, tongue is where the rasa—or juice—flows from.

Failing and Falling

Michel Chaouli

Failing and falling, falling and failing: only a small gap divides the two, the gap that separates the stem of the first instance of the letter 'I' from its dot. But what divides also connects. Close that gap with the mere hint of a stroke, and you have turned *failing* into *falling*. With another stroke, wipe off a patch in that 'l' and *falling* is *failing* once more. The stroke that divides *failing* and *falling*, the stroke that also links them, is a stroke of luck. It's lucky that the English language pairs these two words. Thanks to an accident of linguistic history the two look like twins. I couldn't have started quite this way in another language that I know. But it is a happy accident.

So happy is the accident that *failing* and *falling* look and behave like each other's shadows that the greater wonder may be that not every language links them this way. Do the two not belong to one another? Is it not true that for all of us—for you and for me—failing is, before all else, an instance of falling? And have we not all experienced falling first as a failure? Look online at the countless videos of toddlers struggling to rise. They come up halfway, before falling to the floor; then they do it again and again, falling and rising, falling and rising, and once they have come to a stand, the same thing starts over with the first steps they take. You know scenes like this. You have seen them; more important: you have lived them.

Failing and falling, then, are joined not just because of a fluke of English spelling, but because they are grounded in a fundamental physical condition that permeates human life and human existence.

We live our lives pulled to the ground and pushing from it, somewhere between heaven and earth. Pulling and pushing unfortunately do not hold one another in balance, allowing us to dwell in a state of suspended hovering; that's reserved for the gods, for their messengers, and their various assistants (*Figure 1*). They know how to approach the ground to within an inch without touching it, teasing gravity itself (*Figure 2*). We earthlings, on the other hand, fly economy. We know rough landings. We tend to find ourselves in a burdensome, often inelegant, and sometimes violent tangle with gravity.

Our aspirations aim high; our cultural norms point upwards; we reach for heaven or at least for outer space, but without fail heaviness weighs us down. Everything we do happens on this field of unseen forces fighting it out. Even the most commonplace acts are not exempt: right now, as I am sitting in my chair, you are probably sitting in yours, staring at words just as I am. It doesn't look like much of an accomplishment, yet neither of us would stay sitting were it not for the ceaseless chatter of sensors, nerve fibres, synapses, vestibular systems, and muscles holding you up. In no waking moment are we far from falling. Even in our sleep we manage to fall.

Figure 1: Venus

Figure 2: Superman

It is no surprise, then, how many of our cultural achievements rely on defying gravity. This is especially evident in feats of athleticism. Sometimes, say, in weightlifting, they take a brute-force approach, holding high what by all rights belongs on the ground, and since no practical aim is being served here, the purpose must lie in the fact that gravity itself has been denied its rights. At other times human beings build for themselves a launching pad that, like the magic carpet of fairy tales, carries them over the clouds and across the sky (*Figure 3*). Or take a gymnast: the body finds ways of moving with such

Figure 3: Skateboarder

Figure 4: Gymnast

disregard for the laws of physics that looking at a picture we cannot even tell if it is rising or falling (*Figure 4*). Or, last example, someone manages to take flight, in a way that exceeds utility and necessity: there are easier ways of scoring a basket (*Figure 5*). Everything in this gesture signals superabundance: of strength, beauty, boldness, insouciance. There is more of it all than what is needed to get the job done, which makes the gesture into a gift, a pure gift, and lucky are those who were there to receive it.

How does this relate to falling and failing? I've said that the two maintain an intimate relationship; they are not identical, true, but they do keep close company. Which is why the measure of success, the obverse of failing, often amounts to the obverse of falling—to counteracting falling, overcoming it, even mocking it. The examples I have given bear this out, and we can easily add many more from different spheres of life. Whether it's children doing ballet or NASA putting men on the moon, in one way or the other these undertakings celebrate the defeat of—at least the temporary relief from—gravity, from falling.

Figure 5: Basketball

So intimately is failure understood to be aligned with falling, and success with its opposite, that a whole cottage industry of thinkers has made it its business to understand human beings through the single fact of the vertical posture. You know the idea: basically it asserts that the upright gait makes the human being. You also know that this can be metaphysical hocus-pocus, and immodest, self-serving hocus-pocus at that, even dangerous hocus-pocus, for the idea is often used to bolster the claim of dominion over the horizontally postured inhabitants of the earth. Besides, it's not even consistently applied: among the thinkers who claim that overcoming gravity licenses human supremacy, I have come across few—none, actually—who advocate being ruled by bats or birds.

I say this to give you fair warning that I nonetheless plan to stay with this idea, at least for the duration of this essay. My justification is this: just because some versions of an idea amount to hocus-pocus does not mean that the whole idea is rotten. In fact, my sense is that this idea, rightly handled, opens our view to the intricate ways that failing and falling are entangled. It shows how this entanglement gives us purchase on some of the most significant modes of experience, among these the experience of encountering literature, of significant things generally. These things are not significant per se, but become significant to us when we fall for them and when they befall us. Which only works if we are in a position *from which* to fall, namely up and off the ground. I'll return to this idea, but first I ask you to spend some time in the company of the philosopher Johann Gottlieb Fichte. This is not something you do every day, I assume, and for good reason, since it is a decidedly mixed pleasure. But it turns out one can learn a thing or two from dead white men.

Go back for a moment to the childhood experience that virtually everyone has had, the experience of trying and failing to rise to one's feet. It is not always easy to see why children are so determined to achieve this feat, since most are agile enough on all fours. Philosophers tend to see in such effort a display of the indomitable human urge to break the shackles of gravity and take an upright posture. Let other creatures seek the safety and stability of crawling and slithering: human beings leave all that behind to rise, to raise themselves up. It is a heroic account, and everything that distinguishes human beings—power, knowledge, skills, technology—is thought to depend on the move out of the crouch and into uprightness. Of the many thinkers and writers who have commented on it, let me quote just one, the very Fichte I mentioned, in a book he published two hundred odd years ago (in 1796):

> I hold that the [human] species has freely lifted itself up from the earth and thus acquired for itself the power of looking around in every direction and of surveying one half of the universe in the skies, whilst the animal is by its position chained to the soil which brings forth its nourishment.[1]

This is just the kind of talk that we are tempted to dismiss as an expression of human-centred arrogance. Still, look how much Fichte draws from this one quotidian moment of getting to one's feet. Rising up, the human being raises itself above the animals, literally and figuratively, earning a warrant for dominion over the earth and the creatures that remain bound to it—at the very least, granting itself such a warrant. But Fichte's first concern is not power, but knowledge, for by his lights it is from knowledge that power flows. Before ruling over the earth, human beings look around and observe, for which they need to be upright. The straight back holds the head high, which lets the eye scan the heavens.

This is not an argument about the quantity of knowledge. The idea is not that, being upright, we humans see more and hear more, and hence can know more. Fichte's point is larger and deeper than that. The animal's gaze is bound to the ground, he tells us, one eye on its prey, the other on its predator, while the eye of the human being remains free. Free in what way? Free to look around, free to gaze at the sky, free to take in half the universe, and if you know you are looking at half of something, it means you're free to imagine the other half, and thus free to think the entire universe. Consider for a moment the audacity of this thought: the human being staggers

[1] J.G. Fichte, *The Science of Rights*, translated by A.E. Kroeger (London: Truebner & Co., 1889), p. 123. I have modified the translation throughout.

to his or her feet, and by this act brings all there is within reach of thinking.

If we follow Fichte's train of thought, we begin to see that the downward gaze of the animal and the upward gaze of the human being do not merely fix different objects, the source of nourishment here, the sky there; no, they embody entirely different forms of gazing. One is bound by earthly necessity, the other free to roam the compass of the world. Even when they do focus on the same object, they see different things, because they go about the act of looking differently. In standing up to gravity, what matters is not that the total stock—the quantity—of what can be known grows (assuming even that it does grow: it is easy to forget that by raising ourselves up we lose sight of things the animal knows intimately). What matters, rather, is the change in the quality of what can be known and the manner of knowing. The animal's way of seeing is confined by instinct and shaped by the pressures of life. Human beings, however, Fichte suggests, once vertical, are in a position, again literally and figuratively, to behold the heavens not with an eye to putting it to practical use (say, to orient themselves), but as a phenomenon worthy of observation, contemplation and reflection.

These modes of looking—observation, contemplation and reflection—remove the object from the network of use and consumption in which it is enmeshed on the ground. Observation opens it to an open-ended curiosity. Contemplation lingers with the object for the sake of pleasure or understanding or both. And in reflection the gaze aimed at the stars bends back to include the stargazer, not as yet another object within the cone of vision but as what gives shape to this cone. In this conception, the look of the upright human being, unlike the look of the animal, includes itself; it includes the place from which it looks and the fact of this looking. Which is how human beings can come to ponder their place in a cosmic order. Myth, cosmology, religion, philosophy, science—they open as modes of relating to the world when the heavens come into view as a source of wonder and perplexity.

You may think you are looking at (or remembering) a baby teetering and tottering, yet now you see that you are in fact beholding a human being raise itself into philosophy. But if that is so, then a fall is far worse than a mere failure, since the human being falling out of its upright position falls not to the ground but into animality, into ignorance and bondage.

I started with the child rising and then tumbling as the primordial case of falling and failing, primordial because it is lodged in one of the earliest moments in our lives. Yet as much as this experience is each of ours—nobody can fall in my stead—this moment is not ours alone, part of a personal biography, but marks also the earliest point of the biography of the human species. That is something Fichte insists on. Here is what he writes just before the passage I quoted earlier:

> The question has been asked: Was man intended to walk upright or on four feet? I believe he was not intended to do either. It was left to man as species to choose its mode of motion. A human body can run on four feet; and men grown up amongst animals have so run with incredible swiftness. I hold that *the species* has freely lifted itself up from the earth ... [emphasis added][2]

This is a case of a double origin, then, of ontogeny repeating phylogeny: by Fichte's thinking, each child straining to rise re-enacts a movement performed by the entire human species. But that, in turn, means that every sway and wobble is not the child's alone but repeats humanity's swaying and wobbling. When the child falls, it takes the human species down with it. Which also means that the birth of the human being—the birth of the individual and the birth of the species—happens not when the baby is pressed out of the mother's womb, but when the child pushes herself up and stands on her own two feet, however unsteadily. Since, as Fichte insists, its mode of locomotion is a matter of its own free choice, the human being is not born but gives birth to itself. You see that the snake is biting its own tail: to be free, the human species needs to raise itself off the ground, but to raise itself off the ground, it must be free already.

---

[2] Fichte, *The Science of Rights*.

This again makes us wonder about falling and failing: many things fall—keys, spectacles, rocks, buildings, snowflakes—and in falling they exhibit the triumph of gravity and the failure of anti-gravity, but they do not usually pull down with themselves an entire species or class of things. There is something about the fall of the child, hence about the fall of the human species, that is both less and more than a mere failure. We can turn this idea around: the child can only fall the way human beings fall, because human beings get themselves into a place that makes a fall possible.

If you want a burlesque version of this idea, turn to Plato's dialogue *Theaetetus*, where Socrates recounts the story of Thales, the famed mathematician and astronomer. So absorbed is he in studying the stars, that he promptly falls into a pit. A servant girl, who is watching this, laughs at him: how does he expect to comprehend the world above when he cannot even see what lies inches before him? But Socrates wears the mockery, and the fall, as a badge of honour. 'The same jest,' he says, 'applies to all who pass their lives in philosophy.'[3] You only fall the way Thales falls when you have glimpsed the universe in the sky, when you have faced the mystery and sublimity of the heavenly bodies, and when your gaze has bent back upon itself to include the place from which you gaze and the act of gazing itself. No wonder you overlook the pit by your feet and fall. But so what? The ignorant may regard that fall as a failure when in fact it is an index of your achievement.

One noteworthy thing about this anecdote is how it brims with aggressive laughter. The servant girl is not the only one who laughs: her ridicule is met by Thales's retaliatory laughter—real laughter, not pretend-laughter, Socrates insists (174d)—a laughter meant to signal how utterly insignificant the cares of the common people seem to him. What to make of this dueling hilarity? It alerts us to the link between falling and failing and laughing. We all know that comedy is culturally highly specific, more so than other genres. Jokes tend to die in transit. Yet the humour in falling—a mysterious form of

[3] Plato, *Theaetetus*, 174a, Plato in Twelve Volumes, Vol. 12, translated by Harold N. Fowler (Cambridge, MA, Harvard University Press; London, William Heinemann Ltd, 1921).

humour—seems to defy this truth. The pratfall—falling on your rear end—may be the closest thing we have to a globally cherished prank. Do we laugh to acknowledge how fragile our place is in the world? Were that so, how apt it would be, since laughing, like the fall that prompts it, is available only to those creatures who have loosened their entanglement with the world. Only human beings laugh, and only human beings fall.

You may think that Fichte's account puts too great a stock in linking high-minded human capacities such as freedom and reason to the upright posture, and you would be right. In this, he echoes the many thinkers who have put forward similar ideas. Yet he is unusual in acknowledging, at least implicitly, the intimacy that exists between rising and falling. Yes, the human species, as Fichte puts it, 'lifts up its life into the region of light; it keeps fleeing the earth, which it touches with the least possible part of his body',[4] but it does so forever shadowed by the risk of falling. What is more, it is this risk that even makes the move into the light possible. Look at what Fichte writes:

> Through its daring gait, which is an everlasting expression of its boldness and its skill in observing its balance, [the human species] continually keeps its free will and reason in practice, always remains a *becoming*, and expresses this, his character.[5]

The human gait is daring, Fichte says, an expression of boldness. Why daring, and why bold? We know the answer: because with every step, human beings risk falling. Actually, that gives the risk and the boldness too little credit: this risk is not a regrettable side effect of walking, something that might ideally be managed away, since to take a step, we *need* to jolt our already shaky position on two feet, dislodge one of the two pillars of our stability, which is really a fragility, and throw our whole frame into even greater imbalance. To walk, to dance, to skip, to run is to run a risk, not because you *might* fall, but because to walk, dance, skip or run you

---

[4] Plato, *Theaetetus*, 174a.

[5] Plato, *Theaetetus*, 174a.

must let yourself fall. 'Walking,' Arthur Schopenhauer has said, 'is a continuously checked falling.'[6] There is nothing inevitable about the human species raising itself up; it is not our destiny, Fichte insists, nor our instinct. We *could* stay on all fours, safe and sound on the ground. Yet we try and try again, suffering one setback after the other, just so we can fall prey to the hazards of falling, to become *im*balanced enough to go for a stroll, dash for a bus, kick a ball, or decide to waltz.

You will have noticed that I have been talking more about falling and less about failing. At the outset, I said that failing and falling are joined in our earliest experience of getting off the ground, both as individuals and as a species. But as we have followed this train of thought, it has become clear that, though one is never far from the other, they do not coincide. There are ways of falling that are not simply ways of failing. They are, rather, ways of being, ways of experiencing the world and acting in it. If Fichte, like much of the tradition of philosophy and anthropology to which he belongs, considers the act of raising oneself into the vertical as the moment that the human being steps out of the tangle of natural causes and into the freedom of beholding a world—of *having* a world—then falling does not simply cancel this act, rendering it a mere failure. Falling has its own texture and truth. It opens ways of experience and discloses the world in its own way.

Falling as a way of being—a way that courts failure without succumbing to it—describes some of the most significant experiences we human beings have, including the experience of encountering a work of literature, a painting or a film. When you read a novel or watch a movie, you engage in an intricate dance of activity and passivity: your experience of reading or watching or listening places you into the passive role of someone who endures the feelings and impressions that others bring about in you. You might be amused or absorbed, bored or dismayed: either way, you believe to have suffered these feelings. Yet you also know how much practice and preparation

[6] Arthur Schopenhauer, *The World as Will and Representation*, Vol. 1, translated by Judith Norman and others (Cambridge, UK: Cambridge University Press, 2010), pp. 337–8.

go into reading and watching and listening, how much you need to *do* to be affected and moved in the right sort of way. If we sought to grasp this ambiguous zone between activity and passivity, we could hardly do better than reach for the experience of falling as we have been following it here.

The philosopher Maurice Merleau-Ponty offers an analogy apropos of a different sort of falling. What happens, he asks, when I try to fall asleep? Other than in exceptional cases, I am not felled by sleep against my volition, nor can I, as insomniacs can attest, simply will its arrival. Instead I put myself into a position in which I may receive sleep. It is an important feature of Merleau-Ponty's thinking that this getting-into-position involves both the body—how and where and with whom I lie down—and the mind—how well I am able to keep my demons at bay. True, I do not put myself to sleep, but rather *fall* asleep, which registers this loss of willing and control. Yet I do not usually fall asleep the way that a brick falls to the ground; rather, I *allow* myself to fall, I put myself into a place so that this falling can befall me. This getting-into-the-right-place or getting-into-position is itself not something that just happens to me, but is rather something I need to learn. In fact, it can take years of practice—of finding the right rituals, clutching the right objects, drifting into the right reveries—to learn to do something as seemingly simple and natural as falling asleep. Some of us, perhaps most of us, never master it.

Falling asleep, falling in love, falling in step, falling into error, falling into place, falling in line, falling for a man or for a woman or for a story—are these ways of failing? No doubt they maintain a kinship with failing, distinguished from it by a mere stroke of luck. It is likely true of all human ways of being that they remain cheek to jowl with failure. Yet it is just this kinship that falling keeps with failing that allows it to open to us daring ways of being.

Notes on the Contributors

Clancy Martin is University of Missouri Curators' Professor of Philosophy and Professor of Philosophy at Ashoka University. He writes essays, memoir and fiction. His most recent book is a new translation of and commentary on Nietzsche's *Thus Spoke Zarathustra*.

Ranajit Das is a Bengali poet who has published twelve poetry collections, two collections of literary essays and one novel. Among the many accolades he has received is the Rabindra Puraskar. He has a B.Sc, worked in the state civil service, now retired. He lives in Kolkata.

Lydia Davis is the author of one novel and eight collections of stories, including most recently *Our Strangers* (Bookshop Editions), as well as two collections of non-fiction, *Essays One* (FSG, 2019) and *Essays Two* (FSG, 2021). She has won awards for her translations of works from the French which include Flaubert's *Madame Bovary* (Viking Penguin, 2010) and Proust's *Swann's Way* (Viking Penguin, 2002), and has also translated from other languages, most notably the very short stories of the Dutch writer A.L. Snijders (*Night Train*, New Directions, 2021). Among other honours, she was awarded a MacArthur Fellowship in 2003, both the Award of Merit from the American Academy of Arts and Letters and the Man Booker International Prize in 2013 for her fiction and, in 2020, the PEN/Malamud Award for Excellence in the Short Story. She has been decorated as both Chevalier and Officer of the Order of Arts and Letters by the French government for her fiction and translation. She lives in upstate New York.

Tiffany Atkinson is a poet and critic based in Norwich, UK. Her most recent poetry collection, *Lumen* (Bloodaxe, 2021), was a Poetry Book Society Recommendation and winner of The Medicine Unboxed Creative Prize. She received the Cholmondeley Award for Poetry in 2022. She is currently working on a fifth poetry collection, and completing a monograph entitled *O What Can I Say: Poetry, Ethics and Embarrassment*, for which she received a Leverhulme Research Fellowship. She is Professor of Creative Writing (Poetry) at the University of East Anglia.

Anurag Kashyap is an award-winning film-maker and actor. He is the recipient of four Filmfare Awards and a BAFTA nomination, and has served on the jury of several international film festivals, including the Venice Film Festival and the Sundance Film Festival. In 2013, the Government of France made him a Knight of the Order of Arts and Letters.

Amit Chaudhuri edits Literary Activism.

Sunetra Gupta is a novelist and Professor of Theoretical Epidemiology at the University of Oxford with an interest in infectious diseases. She has been awarded the Scientific Medal by the Zoological Society of London and the Royal Society Rosalind Franklin Award for her scientific research. Her novels have been awarded the Sahitya Akademi Award, the Southern Arts Literature Prize, shortlisted for the Crossword Award, and longlisted for the Orange Prize and the DSC Prize for South Asian Literature. She is a Fellow of the Royal Society of Literature.

Sumana Roy is the author of two works of non-fiction: *How I Became a Tree* and *Provincials: Postcards from the Peripheries*; *Plant Thinkers of Twentieth-Century Bengal*, a work of literary criticism; *Missing: A Novel*; *My Mother's Lover and Other Stories*; and two collections of poems, *Out of Syllabus* and *VIP: Very Important Point.*

Michel Chaouli is author of *Something Speaks to Me: Where Criticism Begins*, *Thinking with Kant's Critique of Judgment*, and other books and articles. He is Professor of German and of Comparative Literature at Indiana University Bloomington where he directs the Center for Theoretical Inquiry in the Humanities.

OTHER TITLES IN THE LITERARY ACTIVISM SERIES

Book of Rahim & Other Poems by Arvind Krishna Mehrotra

On Being Indian by Amit Chaudhuri

Against Storytelling edited by Amit Chaudhuri

Treasurer of Piggy Banks by Vinod Kumar Shukla, translated by Arvind Krishna Mehrotra

Memories of Rain by Sunetra Gupta